Practical Anarchism

"A joyful rethinking of anarchism. Branson draws on a wealth of cutting-edge theory and the messiness of activism to illuminate new ways to transform society. The result is a practical guide to everyday revolutions. A real treasure."
—Alex Prichard, author of *Anarchism: A Very Short Introduction*

"A clever, inspiring and accessible book! Branson's brilliant method of weaving together our collective and individual lives alongside our most complex relationships with the many (eco) systems that we are part of is truly refreshing and ground-breaking. I feel that I and many other radicals have walked the edges of so many of these conversations that Branson has skillfully and necessarily busted open. I sure wish I had read this book years ago, but other than that, I will share it with everyone I know! And especially with anyone who has ever told me my ideas were impractical and pie-in-the-sky naivety."
—carla joy bergman, editor of *Trust Kids!* and co-author of *Joyful Militancy: Building Thriving Resistance in Toxic Times*

"Scott Branson denaturalizes property and hierarchy in every dimension of human life. Steeped in historical and archival knowledge of Black and queer proletarian feminisms and decolonial struggles against the state, *Practical Anarchism* is a powerful guide to the collective manufacture of utopia now."
—Sophie Lewis, author of *Abolish the Family: A Manifesto for Care and Liberation*

"Scott Branson confidently weaves political theory into everyday practice to expose the affinities between anarchism and contemporary anti-oppression politics and closes the gap between imagined futures and their creation. *Practical Anarchism* presents clear, astute critiques of work, school, and the destruction of community in capitalism, and serves as a handbook for liberation, both gently optimistic and intensely motivating."
—Ruth Kinna, author of *The Government of No One: The Theory and Practice of Anarchism*

"Anarchism's record as a political movement might be shaky. We have seen no large-scale, long-term anarchist society. Yet, anarchism's record as an ethical guideline stands tall. Time and time again, anarchists have been involved in improving social relationships, empowering dispossessed and marginalized communities, and supporting struggles on the right side of history. In this highly readable and passionate book, Scott Branson sheds a light on many examples of everyday anarchist engagement and its rich contribution to making the world a better place."
—Gabriel Kuhn, author of *Soccer vs. the State: Tackling Football and Radical Politics*

"*Practical Anarchism* hands us an anarchist kaleidoscope, inviting us to shake up this world and see the endless array of beautiful possibilities that are already present in the here and now. It offers this delightful gift not so that we may view an infinity of ever-shifting promise as mere spectators but rather as a reminder that we ourselves are continually engaged in creating collective care and freedom. It's what I'd call 'everyday anarchism'—the making and doing, routinely, of lives worth living for everyone. This book—tender, dreamy, actionable—inspires us to pick up all the sparkly, even if sometimes jagged, edges of daily life that too often go unnoticed and toss them, time and again, into utopian play."
—Cindy Barukh Milstein, author of *Try Anarchism for Life: The Beauty of Our Circle*

"Deftly and joyfully shows us that lives lived with compassion and collective autonomy in the engagements we call anarchy have practical applications in our everyday living individually and collectively."
—scott crow, insurgent, author of *Black Flags and Windmills: Hope, Anarchy and the Common Ground Collective*

"Scott Branson offers a unique and much-needed intervention in traditional anarchist thought to argue that anarchism—whether it's identified as such or not—is a seed in most of our liberation practices and ideas. Their perspective comes from radical organizing experience, rigorous study of critical race and queer theory, as well as their commitment to their relationships and communities. Weaving practical advice alongside women of color, queer activists, abolitionists, and more, Branson offers us a beautiful reminder that we do anarchism everyday—through care, through imagining, through loving—against and in spite of the state. In a moment where it is easy to feel hopeless, *Practical Anarchism* is a fresh and unique take on how creating new worlds free of hierarchy and domination is a practice we're already doing. And Branson offers us the tools to help it grow. This brilliant book is an antidote to giving up."
—Raechel Anne Jolie, author of *Rust Belt Femme*

Practical Anarchism
A Guide for Daily Life

Scott Branson

PLUTO  PRESS

First published 2022 by Pluto Press
New Wing, Somerset House, Strand, London WC2R 1LA
and Pluto Press Inc.
1930 Village Center Circle, Ste. 3-384, Las Vegas, NV 89134

www.plutobooks.com

British Library Cataloguing in Publication Data
A catalogue record for this book is available from the British Library

ISBN   978 0 7453 4493 5   Hardback
ISBN   978 0 7453 4492 8   Paperback
ISBN   978 0 7453 4496 6   PDF
ISBN   978 0 7453 4494 2   EPUB

This book is printed on paper suitable for recycling and made from fully managed and
sustained forest sources. Logging, pulping and manufacturing processes are expected
to conform to the environmental standards of the country of origin.

Typeset by Stanford DTP Services, Northampton, England

Simultaneously printed in the United Kingdom and United States of America

Contents

Introduction

The true focus of revolutionary change is never merely the oppressive situations that we seek to escape, but that piece of the oppressor which is planted deep within each of us, and which knows only the oppressors' tactics, the oppressors' relationships.

Audre Lorde, "Age, Race, Class, and Sex: Women Redefining Difference"

How to Survive the Future

The main argument of this book is that anarchism is a name for something most of us already do. The name itself matters less than the doing. In writing this book, my objective is to reach out to those of you who haven't already developed tactics of survival and interdependence, or who haven't yet recognized the rebellion that you already live every day. In a simple way, my argument for anarchism is a process of denaturalizing all the aspects that structure our lives in ways that seem unquestionable, and reframing ways of relating to the people in our lives and the world that surrounds us from the point of view of care and freedom. While anarchism as a political ideological term has a recent and European origin, the ways of living that anarchism describes have long been practiced in various places, to varying degrees, throughout history and beyond. Those histories get buried in attempts to naturalize a view of the "human" that needs hierarchy, order, control, domination, and security. The truth that many anarchist writers have already tried to show over the years is that when it comes down to it, people tend to organize themselves quite well without domination and hierarchy. It takes a certain amount of (constant, everyday) violence to maintain the power structures of the state, the market, and gendered, racialized, and sexual differences, which make us feel dependent on answers coming from above.

The feeling that we need this kind of reorganizing of our lives is pretty dire, as the effects of the climate crisis get worse every year. Optimistic targets of cutting down emissions endorsed by state institutions and corporations seem less and less likely to be achieved, or worse, are proven to be insufficient to halt a world structure that is already collapsing. As the author of the anarchist text *Desert* claims, we cannot anticipate a worldwide revolution that will overthrow state and capital and therefore save us from climate catastrophe. But there is still space within this crumbling edifice of Western civilization to reassert other ways of life; ways that would allow us a different kind of freedom than that promised by consumer choice, electoral politics, and (unreachable) wealth accumulation.

One of my repeated ideas in this book is that anarchism proposes ways to break up with forms that don't work, that cause harm, that have failed. On the flipside of this, the state and the market try to position themselves as eternal, as the culmination of human history, as the solution to all the "problems" of inhabiting earth over thousands of years. This answer gets naturalized for us in the way that the state intercedes in all of our relationships, whether through recording our demographic data, centralizing access to services, or policing and surveilling us. We defer to an authority to solve our problems, and that feels normal. Anarchism instead looks for more direct ways to solve problems, to work in the places where conflicts and problems arise, rather than outsourcing our solutions to authoritarian structures that are as likely to cause further harm as provide any meager aid. We might find that it is actually more time-consuming, and less successful, if we don't directly confront the conflicts in our lives, but call on authority to intervene. But overall, engaging in conflict with the people we love, with whom we share space or collaborate on projects of any kind—this is a form of care that we need to prioritize. An anarchist approach to daily life starts in this form of care, taking care of all the life around us, whether "human" or "more than human" (animals, plants, ecosystems in general). And an essential part of care is acknowledging the limits of our capacity and facing up to the difficult moments of living together.

This book proposes a way to infuse your daily life with anarchism by asking you to disidentify with the power structures that determine your life, which so often are internalized unconsciously and manifest in even the most mundane aspects of our living. Ongoing work is needed to unplug ourselves from the dominant world order, to unlearn oppressive masculinity, to betray and destroy white supremacy, and to remove ourselves from the logic of the state and the market that determines our interactions with each other through individual gain, competition, and the idea of protecting ourselves from one another. This book intends to guide us on this project, as the project of anarchism, to undo the hierarchies and stop our own reproduction of their logics in our daily lives.

Historically, anarchism is a revolutionary political ideology developed in the nineteenth century, in the contexts of debates around socialism, communism, and the labor movement, to aim for a stateless society, ordered around mutual aid and individual autonomy. Anarchism counters all forms of hierarchy, so we can extend its critique of the state and capitalism to other ways that power and oppression are imposed: by the means of race, gender, sexuality, citizenship status, childhood, and so on. Often we hear the proposition of anarchism as a utopian ideal set forever in the future: after the revolution, perhaps we will be able to achieve a society without rulers, where people can determine their own lives individually and collectively. However, just as prison and police abolitionists point out that abolition isn't an end goal but a daily endeavor of creating the world we want, anarchism too uses the idea of "prefiguration," which means living anarchism today, creating that better world even in the face of state oppression, racial capitalist exploitation, imperial wars, environmental collapse, cisheteropatriarchy, and the other hierarchical principles that determine our lives. It's not a wish for collapse or a passive or messianic awaiting of the revolution. Instead, this anarchism acts now to build relationships of care.

Of course, the anarchist will also look for direct confrontation with the systems of power that hoard resources and impose hierarchy. This is the more familiar anarchist, masked and dressed in black, breaking corporate windows (an echo of the image of the anarchist a century ago, mustachioed and holding a bomb). But perhaps the embodied lesson we can take from direct-action-oriented anarchism, which has played an extensive role in the current manifestation of uprisings that swell street protest movements, is the building of relationships during a heightened moment of struggle. Just as in the face of climate disasters, people come together to aid each other's survival; when facing a police line among anarchists, you can feel what it is like to have someone get your back.

But what do we do when we aren't in the streets in direct confrontation? This book suggests we might find a similar mode of relationship that arises spontaneously in the face of crisis by rethinking how we relate to power structures, rooting out the logics of hierarchy that predetermine our judgments, and reorienting our connections with people through support for mutual responsibility and individual autonomy. I will enter into anarchism from this point to argue that we are not trying to "achieve" anarchism, for it's an endless process, one we might just as well call "living." I want to draw our attention to all the ways that we haven't been completely conquered, disciplined, and ordered into a way of life that naturalizes hierarchy, violence, competition, and mass death.

In this book, I bring a feminist and queer perspective to anarchism, particularly building from the work of Black feminism, and Indigenous and decolonial feminisms, to suggest that the chance of anarchism already exists in so many ways that we may not be aware of, and when we start to shift the kaleidoscope in this manner, we can maximize our anarchist ways of relating and living together. Even more, I think that by relating to our lives through daily anarchism, a comprehensive disidentification with the ways—particularly in a Euro-American context—that we have been trained to behave, we can start to bring together the moments of joy and freedom and refuse to place ourselves in our own subjection. Joy and freedom, like anarchism, I contend, are momentary experiences. We can't access a perfect life once and for all, and we can never be assured that we have arrived: as Ursula K. Le Guin writes about anarchism in her novel, *The Dispossessed*, when we "demand security, a guarantee," of that world, if it is "granted, [it] would become a prison." In this way, anarchism has to be a continual practice, not a static ideology, not a map towards revolution, not a blueprint of a post-revolutionary society. Anarchism only occurs in practice, as we continually interrogate and reflect on the ways that power inheres in centers and corners, and we diffuse that power towards collective care and self-determination.

In revolutionary thinking, there is often an emphasis placed on the more glamorous (read masculinist) aspects of struggle, from direct action to guerrilla warfare, leaving out both the work done to make that struggle possible and the life that it supposedly aims to enable. This is where the feminist lens is essential: we always have to acknowledge that any direct conflict with the state, with the boss, with the masters, and with fascists, is made possible by the baseline of care we need to live. Here, I take my cue from the seventies feminist manifesto by Silvia Federici, *Wages against Housework*, which argues that demanding wages for the labor expected for free from women under the guise of love, marriage, and motherhood is the first step towards refusing the role. It's a transformative project: "We want to call work what is work so that eventually we may discover what is love and create what will be our sexuality which we have never known." This line will become a refrain for the book, as I want to argue that if we find anarchism in our daily life, we may just be able to discover what living is.

Each chapter of this book will take as its focus an aspect of daily life, from relationships and activities, like family and work, to the seemingly rigid contours of our lives, like time and space. In this book, I suggest that practical anarchism, a practice of daily life, entails a process of disidentification with inherited and ingrained cultural logics that naturalize the lives we are living under state and capital, regimes of racial oppression and genocide, compulsory labor and nuclear families, and so on. A simple reduction of all these logics might come down to the fact that many of our cultural positions allow us to think that some people are better than others and that some people don't deserve to live (or they don't deserve food, shelter, and care). This hierarchical distinction among people gets naturalized and threaded through the very infrastructure of the modern nation state, through the racialization of particular groups, through the gender distinctions that keep all women in subjugation and maintain trans people as deviant, through the borders and citizenship status that manage the flow of labor and capital, through the ownership of property and the idea that we should owe a landlord or the bank for our homes while some people don't deserve homes, through the idea that children aren't full human beings yet and are under complete dominance of their adult caretakers and basically any adult who might step into that role. The result is that dominance and control are everyday aspects of the world we inhabit, such that they pass most often without notice.

Disidentification means looking at the ideas we take for granted—what Marxists might call ideology; the ways that we are positioned within our language, culture, and political and economic framework to perform specific roles—and asking whom these ideas serve. Can we rethink these ideas from the angle of sharing power and resources, promoting collective freedom, operating through care? In each chapter, I focus on the ways specific activities and relationships are naturalized in our lives and suggest ways that we can unearth the power structures so that we can stop living our lives according to pathways that lead both to our own subjugation and our own attempts to hold power over others. In a sense, the process entails uprooting our own sense of our selves—our identities—since we form ourselves within the framework of the systems of power that are taught and embodied in our families, as well as in our education. However, I show that in many ways the process of disidentification puts us in touch with ways of relating to each other and the world that had to be intentionally destroyed by our indoctrination into these cultures of power. In other words, we typically want to help each other out, we get a feeling of joy of connection, we have curiosity about the world, its details, and its differences; we have to be trained to look out only for ourselves even to the extent of causing harm to others. In the end, we don't even know what we could be, alone and together.

The tactic of disidentification, as José Esteban Muñoz describes it in *Disidentifications,* can be traced to Black and women of color feminisms as well as queer modes survival; in other words, it develops from a minoritized position that has to negotiate with the structures of power that doom that position to destruction. Rather than choosing between assimilating (playing along) or simply forming an oppositional identity, disidentification works as a way outside this false choice, outside of the realm of purity of opposition, to try to survive and thrive beyond the structure we currently inhabit, without buying into the systems that want to kill us. In altering our relationships to ourselves, each other, and the world, we can perhaps reproduce a different set of relations than the dominant order: another kind of world.

Disidentification, therefore, isn't simply a negative program, but entails a reorientation towards the coordinates of our lives. In each chapter, I use a mode of disidentification to rethink the things we take for granted in our life, and in the process I open up space to reframe these ways of living from an anarchist perspective, that is, a perspective that aims for collective liberation, mutual aid, and self-determination. We can't wait for the perfect moment to start living; we can't expect a pure revolutionary change in which we leave the old world behind for good. We have to work with what is in front of us; we have to prepare ourselves to live lives that promote our freedom and everyone else's too. We must refuse their terms, but we can use the resources at hand to re-envision what life could really be.

Chapter Overview

Chapter 1 gives an overview of the ideas associated with anarchism in order to present a practical understanding of anarchism as a mode of disidentification. When we refuse to cooperate with the hierarchies and binaries that discipline us into our world, we can take a different look at our daily lives and ask ourselves what life really is. Anarchism in the daily mode is rooting out where we let power dictate our relationships and actions; it opens up time and space for us to live otherwise.

Chapter 2 looks at our relationships, from friendship to love to family, proposing that we emphasize our ability to break up, to end things, to set boundaries. In much liberatory discourse, there is always an emphasis on community, but perhaps this idea of community ends up overemphasizing a kind of connection that often feels unattainable. If we start by saying no, we can learn about saying yes, and thereby form the relationships and webs of care that can actually sustain us.

Chapter 3 asks us to disidentify from the moralism of work, to reject competition and thinking our identity is bound with our jobs. Anarchism is anti-work, as a relationship of exploitation under capitalism. One refrain throughout the book is to rethink our ideas of work as labor, in order to reorient towards forms of relating as care. Therefore, we can look at our jobs as places where we can form other relationships and take whatever access we have to resources and share. We aim for a world without work, but what do you do now? If not unionize or collectivize (which are laudable), find ways to collaborate, support, and steal!

Chapter 4 frames our anarchist disidentification with the norms and discipline forced on us through school and education. Rather than look at institutional education as a good in itself, we think of anarchism as a mode of studying the world from a liberatory perspective, an act that helps us refuse to reproduce this system and start making other worlds. We can liberate study from any specific place and see it as a curious relation to our surroundings, done in collectivity with all forms of life.

Chapter 5 takes our orientation towards money as an enforced means of survival and asks us to reject the moralism of earning, saving, and spending. Our relation to the scarcity of money helps reproduce the exploitative conditions of capitalism, which keeps us saving for a someday that will never come. Our anarchism reframes money through spending, waste, luxury, theft, and sharing. Yes, we have to buy things in our current situation—our participation or non-participation in the economy isn't the key point of revolution. Instead, whatever you have, spread it around, think of your spending from the perspective of looting.

Chapter 6 helps us see our daily anarchism as a creative project, not only in our making and enjoying art but in the way we live our daily lives. Anarchism is expressive and visionary. It helps us analyze the images that inundate our lives and question forms of representation that are given to us as modes of liberation. Anarchist art helps inspire us to live out other worlds that don't reproduce our daily misery.

Chapter 7 looks at the spaces where we live, the scale of anarchism, and the ideas of property. We often hear that anarchism won't work because it's not centralized and can't handle the scale of the problems that face the world destroyed by the state and capitalism. But this is a logic of top-down organizing. How do we fend for ourselves? In our reorientation to the dominant modes of living, we see anarchism as cropping up in the interstices: overlapping worlds of care and relation on a small scale within the structures that try to rule our lives. Not every space is under total control, so how can we see ourselves as caring for the land, simultaneously playing guest and host to others.

Chapter 8 proposes our anarchism as fleeting, momentary, and interruptive. We already live anarchy in moments throughout our day. Finding the places of freedom helps us realize how our daily lives and relationships form the world. Anarchism is non-progressive and non-triumphant. We don't expect the revolution, and our failures actually spell our commitment to playing and experimenting everyday anew. From this perspective, we can reorient our anarchism towards the world through loosely linked, momentary experiences of freedom—of life— that speak to the ongoing possibility of living anarchism now.

In the Coda, I try to describe the world outside the state as we currently live it, bringing together some of the key references I've drawn along the way. Practical anarchism lets us see that every day we live moments of freedom that can't be captured, can't be located. This is the life we've never let ourselves know; this is the daily life that springs up to show us the way.

For ease of using this book, at the end of each chapter I have included a two-question FAQs section to try to address the fundamental issues of the subject matter in a more concise way.

* * *

As a final note, I want to acknowledge my own position in writing this. I am writing embedded in my own organizing and community in the southeast of the so-called United States. In clear ways, I am limited by my own perspective, and I take responsibility for anything I left out. I am Jewish and a queer/trans femme. My life has been marked in particular ways by whiteness and patriarchal masculinity. The dominant framework I address is the power structure inherited from European colonialism and slavery, which to a certain extent has been exported around the world but hasn't been imposed evenly, and hasn't fully destroyed the cultural lifeways of Indigenous groups all around the world. But even in the difference between the US and European contexts, I am closer and more informed about the United States. I regularly refer to the dominant ideologies of colonial power and anti-Blackness, which play out differently in different states, but which arguably form the knowledge and structure of modernity. I do not claim expertise or authority, and what I've cobbled together here comes from experiences of collaboration, of studying alongside other people. My work here is fundamentally indebted to the writing of previous thinkers, and I have particularly drawn from the histories of Black feminist, Indigenous, and women of color thought. To keep this book accessible, I have avoided extensive footnotes and scholarly citations, but I name these thinkers and their ideas along the way. Additionally, I have included a short Further Reading section that offers some of the books and writers that have been important to me. Each chapter deals with ideas and topics that could easily make up a book or library on their own. Here, I am distilling a way of thinking about anarchism into an accessible approach to reshaping the contours of our lives. I hope to contribute practical thoughts on how we already express anarchism in our daily lives as a way to move people towards refusing the wages of the good life enshrined in our continual barrage of representations of how we ought to be. Together we can feel our lives for what they are, below the surveilling eyes of the state, of capitalism, of the image, in an embodied movement towards collective liberation.

1

Am I Already Doing Anarchy?
Anarchy on and off the Streets

But was not a theory of which *all* the elements were provably true a simple tautology? In the region of the unprovable, or even the disprovable, lay the only chance for breaking out of the circle and going ahead.
  Ursula K. Le Guin, *The Dispossessed*

- Introduction to anarchism
- Anarchism as a daily practice
- Disidentification and care

What Is Anarchism?

There has been a long propaganda war, arguably one that has already been won, to associate anarchism with chaos, wanton political violence, and general unrest. In part, this association came from the acts of actual anarchists, whose investment in "propaganda by the deed"—actions aimed to show the general population the weak spots in the power systems—included political violence like assassinations and bomb throwing that would lead to bystander deaths. Similar to the way the term "terrorist" has been used since the 1970s (even down to its racialized undertones, since early European anarchists were often ethnic minorities and immigrants in the countries where they organized), anarchist was a term that referred to an unfathomable political agitator who wanted to destroy, embodying an imminent threat to order (or the routine that people often crave). In some places, it even became a crime to identify yourself as an anarchist. I always like to point out that "terror" actually comes from the actions of the state, even though it has come to be used as a label for individual actors—the term traces back to the Reign of Terror, the French Revolution swallowing itself in surveillance, suspicion, and the guillotine. Therefore, the image of the violent anarchist serves as a distraction from the fact that the state and capitalism are conducting an ongoing social war on everyone, the whole planet, and all that lives on it, with particular people bearing the brunt of its most explicit violence. Perhaps many people who have been previously sheltered from this realization may see it more explicitly in the willingness of most states to sacrifice significant numbers of their population for the sake of the market in the recent Covid-19 pandemic. When this social war has become so evidently clear, we can confidently say that now is the best time to start practicing anarchism.

Recently, the term anarchist has come back into fashion, along with domestic terrorist and outside agitator, as a way for the mainstream news and politicians to discredit movements in the street. This negative label usually gets wielded when there has been property destruction during a protest (the often-mentioned Starbucks windows getting smashed, the line being crossed from what is supposedly an acceptable protest towards something that is "violent"—against windows). Or, for example, in the United States, when a Black-led movement offers a revolutionary perspective rather than demands for reform: the acceleration of chaos is the fault of the white anarchist, who comes from outside the community. This strategy has a long history, particularly as a way to discredit radical Black liberation movements going back to early abolitionists. But it's a strategy that works well because we have been taught to associate anarchy with chaos. (Without the state, without the police, we'd have nothing but complete anarchy—this is the argument inherent in the idea of the police-provided "thin blue line" keeping our social order from chaos.) Some anarchists like to argue that there is a difference between "anarchy" and "anarchism": where the former might designate disorder, or even chaos, the second refers to a liberatory perspective outside all forms of domination and hierarchy. In the end, perhaps, we are fighting a losing battle when we remain married to the term, though Marquis Bey argues in *Anarcho-Blackness* for taking it up proudly as a form of deviancy, just as queer people have reclaimed the derogatory term "queer" as a way of marking their rejection of the dominant society.

And yet, anarchism has come back into the limelight as a real idea, a way of organizing, and arguably as a motivating force or ethos behind the worldwide movements that have increasingly emerged over the last two decades in the face of austerity, ecological devastation, authoritarian regimes, colonial extraction, and racist violence. We've seen the media images of anarchists in black bloc, upping the ante of confrontation in the usual rigmarole of street protests; we've seen anarchists creating mutual aid projects in the face of climate disasters; and along with the rise of anti-fascist street movements confronting the worldwide rise of white supremacists, the term anarchism gets freely associated with anything radical. More and more people are experiencing organizing from an anarchist perspective, even if they don't refer to themselves as anarchists. In the moment, on the streets, they participate in non-hierarchical, horizontal, consensus-based work to support movements against capitalism, racism, fascism, colonialism, misogyny, homo/transphobia, and all forms of domination.

Becoming part of a movement, it might seem, involves forms of initiation. Many anarchists made their way into the fold through subcultural routes like punk scenes or radical queer communities. In the end, this kind of entry point creates all manner of obstacles for people to get involved, especially as we are more and more atomized and isolated. Social media gives a potential entry point for learning radical views, but it also runs the risk of trapping people in a cycle of hot takes and denouncements disconnected from real world-building. Add to this a legacy of state repression going back to various laws targeting anarchists (and the successful propaganda mentioned above), and many anarchists tend to be suspicious of newcomers. A huge failure of the movement has been the difficulties it presents to getting involved. My experience as a teacher has been that when I present anarchism to my students, often in the form of science fiction novels that describe anarchistic societies, they quite often say, "well, I guess I'm an anarchist." I find this to be a more encouraging entry point than the gatekeeping of subcultures or the obsessively security-minded groups of well-worn militants. I've had multiple projects derailed by an obsession with security against infiltrators, which ends up simply discouraging new people from collaborating. This viewpoint seems to forget the fact that at some point our action will have to be public and confrontational if we are to make any impact. If we do not connect to other people and their own sense of autonomy and mutual care, we end up talking to a small group of people who already think the same way. Instead, anarchism should give us the means to identify with each other as people in similarly dire circumstances, who are looking for better ways to help themselves and each other.

Too often, anarchism is touted as a white ideology in opposition to Black liberation movements—despite a history of Black anarchism and current innovative and specific iterations of Black anarchism—or as an academic fetish, despite the fact that anarchism has almost no hold in the academy, especially compared to the widespread worship of Marx, who fits much better into an academic tradition. These distortions of anarchism's proponents—as a white elite—is a propaganda move by the actual elite that is clearly self-serving and self-righteous. (This is not at all to say that white-dominated anarchist spaces don't reproduce white supremacy, or that no anarchists maintain elitist, theory-infatuated fixations.) More problematic is the way that anarchism is ensconced in these particular subcultures that might not feel welcoming to people who don't share certain interests or lifestyles. This situation creates a sense of exclusion for a "normal" person who, when exposed to anarchist ideas, suddenly realizes, "maybe I'm an anarchist," because their default way of thinking aligns with anarchist ideas of how to organize daily, communal life, along with a rejection of abuse of power and domination. They just didn't have the particular vocabulary of anarchism, or weren't in the social milieu where it gets identified as such. Or they thought that being an anarchist involves looking or dressing a certain way. Anarchism as an identity, however, is less interesting to me, since it can so often be a fashion statement that actually has nothing to do with a practice that moves towards increasing collective freedom through rethinking relationships and distributing power and resources. In fact, adhering to a fixed conception of what anarchism should look like gets in the way of a flexible anarchism that tries in each moment to reorder the world through care.

Recently, Black liberation thinkers and movement workers, such as Zoé Samudzi and William C. Anderson, have been reclaiming the term anarchism in relation to the conditions of Blackness and colonialism and different histories of liberation work. The legacy of Black liberation and anti-colonial movements also helps show how thinking of anarchism as a narrow ideology (at the very least needing to be named) overlooks the ways that people have organized in non-hierarchical ways over the last century and beyond. If we hold ourselves to a Marxist-type academic standard of attributing anarchist theories to specific theorists, we end up losing sight of anarchism as a continually renewed practice shared by many in their moments of self-determination, especially when these experiences don't follow revolutionary blueprints. Along these lines, Saidiya Hartman's book *Wayward Lives, Beautiful Experiments* creates an archival imagination of Black women at the turn of the twentieth century who lived on the margins, confronting a state set on disposing of them. Hartman conceives her project as seeking "to illuminate the radical imagination and everyday anarchy of ordinary colored girls, which has not only been overlooked, but is nearly unimaginable." Their kind of anarchism not only got them labeled as deviant by the power systems of the time, but was invisible to the originating European theorists of anarchism and their followers. And yet, these queer Black people, while also coming into contact with the violence of the state, found ways to live their daily lives outside the law.

There have already been books making the argument that anarchism encompasses how people tend to organize themselves spontaneously without the intervention of hierarchical structures from the outside, perhaps most famously in Peter Kropotkin's *Mutual Aid: A Factor of Evolution*, which looks at the success of cooperative organization in human and non-human communities. There is a whole anarchist literature that has emerged over more than a century since that argues for the practicality and functionality of anarchism, rather than allowing it to be transformed into an extreme outside chance (utopian vision) or bogeyman of liberal democratic nation states. Anarchism is quickly debunked by a request for proof of an "anarchist society." As David Graeber pointed out, this is a trick question, as typically the doubter wants you to point to something that would end up being an anarchist state, since our minds are so saturated with the state as a marker of culture and identity. This means we overlook not only the temporary constellations of anarchy that have existed throughout (and in some cases predate) recorded history, but the anarchist experiments in larger-scale social organizing that persist despite (or have been crushed by) international capitalist state accord. It means we also overlook the fact that not every corner of our lives is completely ruled by capitalist statist dictates—we all have experience in our everyday lives of doing quite well without the need for politicians, police, and bureaucracy. In fact, we mostly experience the entrance of any of the aforementioned as messing up our usual proceedings. This interstitial space and time is what I want to call the "no place" of anarchism: it exceeds the official recording of history or the geographical contours of mapping, and yet it is the daily experience of most of us, much of the time.

The Occupy era of anarchism showed us some of anarchism's shortcomings as it was being practiced in the moment, in the way a total commitment to consensus in large groups can be hijacked by small factions or even people purposefully trying to derail the process. However, this moment was crucial in introducing anarchism as a practice to many people, which only became strengthened by the following few years of uprisings: in the USA, we saw the Standing Rock encampment to stop the Dakota Access Pipeline and uprisings against police killings of Black people, culminating in movements to resist Trump and his racist, murderous policies. Globally, there have been more and more grassroots movements with significant anarchist participation or anarchistic tendencies, from Chile to Hong Kong, from France to India, from Sudan to Greece, and more. Moreover, this period also saw the incredible spread of mutual aid projects to help communities afflicted by climate catastrophes like hurricanes, flooding, and wildfires. I wrote this book in the immediate wake of the Covid-19 pandemic and George Floyd rebellions, which have further built up anarchist practices of direct action and world-building and helped form a new generation of people looking to non-state, mundane ways of finding freedom—spreading globally from the USA outward through international solidarity.

We are still in this moment, where the legacy of protest movements is entangled with occupations, and there are ongoing mutual aid projects across the world providing people with resources in the face of failed state efforts. Large numbers of people around the world have been forced into direct conflict with the state, regardless of their political ideology, and thus have faced the truth of the state's rule, which involves wanton violence against its own population should they dare to do things for themselves. At the same time, these people, along with people who have been in movements for years, have created more and more infrastructure, networks of care, and relationships of trust, out of necessity and in the face of the inescapable failure of the services we are taught to expect as citizens of a wealthy state.

The contribution I want to make with this additional reframing of anarchism is to focus on anarchism as a daily practice of care, in relationships with our loved ones, ourselves, our comrades in struggle, our neighbors, strangers, and unpredictable solidarities to come. Again, I draw on the amazing recent work of anarchists and abolitionists in this direction, including Mariame Kaba, adrienne maree brown, Leah Lakshmi Piepzna-Samarasinha, Leanne Betasamosake Simpson, and Cindy Milstein.

My own contribution develops out of my own study of these writers, many of whom are (Black and Brown) femmes, a group of people often left out of the mythologizing imagery of the party-minded white cis male-dominated revolutionary left, but who are almost always responsible for the care work that actually allows freedom struggles to continue and the people who actively take it up—or those caught beyond their will in the crosshairs of state violence—to survive. Direct confrontation is the most visible part of anarchism, but daily anarchism happens in communal meals and the sharing of food and necessities, spreading resources through the community, creating plans to support collective and individual mental health, and teaching and learning collaboratively—underground or less visible projects that make life possible within the cracks of a system that is geared towards all of our deaths. While this type of care work is often feminized, I'm by no means suggesting that the most explicitly militant confrontations aren't also led by feminized people. Care work and self-defense go hand in hand. Many of the recent anti-police rebellions have been spurred on by Black (trans) women, and a significant number of Indigenous resistance movements have women at the forefront.

Is Anarchism a Politics?

To highlight care and relationships as the primary terrain of anarchism reframes understanding of anarchism as a question of living rather than a political ideology. This isn't to advocate what gets dismissed as lifestyle anarchism, but to say a truly anarchist perspective on life will utterly shift how you view the world around you and your position within the state and market. One of the major ruses played on us, as second-wave feminism teaches, is the separation of the political from the personal (or private). This gendered division is why feminized labor gets erased. We think of politics as something you do outside of the house, even if it's simply pulling a voting lever every few years, depending on how "involved" you are. Some of us may canvass for politicians or particular issues; it's easy enough to sign petitions, and then we might show up for the demo in our town center, to protest some egregious infraction by those in power. Maybe politics also includes the information on the news and the latest debates in the halls of power. But we separate it from our daily lives.

The classic feminist slogan that "the personal is the political" means that even those aspects of our life that seem completely untouched by state control are still contoured by it some way. The most obvious aspect of this can be seen in terms of people's autonomy over their bodies, with pregnancy, abortion, hormone replacement, and so on reliant on state policies and infrastructure for access (or denial of access). But it can also mean simply the gendered division of labor in the household, particularly cisgender heterosexual households, where a man works a waged or salaried job while the woman might do that kind of work plus the unwaged, unremarked domestic labor of childrearing, shopping, cooking, cleaning, and providing emotional support. The unwaged housework enables the waged work but does not get seen as work—it's naturalized as a moral imperative and demanded in the name of love. We can extend this even further, where waged care work out of the house enables the structures of capitalism to persist, as in the case of educators, healthcare workers, domestic workers, cleaners, and other kinds of caregivers.

But let's flip the old slogan, or at least our understanding of the political. Indeed, let's infuse our entire lives with political meaning, but cease to understand politics as a specialized, meaningful realm to which we relate through critique, participation, reading/knowledge, or even disavowal. Some political theorists trace politics back to the Greek idea of the marketplace as a place for discussion of social and civic matters (whence we get the sense of the marketplace of ideas, although capitalism has infused that with a misleading interpretation of how ideas compete, with the best one winning). The place for political discussion was kept distinct from the home, which therefore was deemed less important. This distinction creates a false fold in our lives where the things beyond the crease only hold individual or even familial meaning, and yet this is precisely where our lives take place. The way we organize our relationships, how we raise children and educate ourselves, and the structures we take on, are all infused with political ideology—and can all be reframed to counter that hierarchical way of thinking. The division of public and private, just like the division between politics and economics, is a political division in itself.

Anarchists, meanwhile, like to distinguish their relationship to action as outside the liberal conception of politics: the public sphere, policy, and bureaucratic management. If politics represents a split in our lives—one wedge of our alienation, just like our work life (inane work for abstract currency)—then we don't want to think about our everyday actions, even those that partake in the long revolutionary struggle to change the world, as politics. For these reasons, anarchists will abjure politics and even the term activism, since these concepts accept the terms and divisions of the structure we are trying to destroy. In a liberated world, these distinctions would be meaningless. We aren't looking for a mere political revolution but a complete social revolution. One commonly referenced example of this erasure of the political distinction is the Black Panther Party's breakfast program. Providing kids with breakfast seems innocuous enough, though obviously necessary. The Panthers knew this basic necessity was just as political as any direct action, firstly because it provided people with what they needed outside the structure of the state, and secondly because it became a space for political practice to be shared and enacted through building community. FBI head J. Edgar Hoover considered the breakfast program to be one of the biggest threats to the US government and its attempt to stop the Panthers, which shows how something as simple as free food can be seen as a direct confrontation with the state.

Many of us may already have come to the realization that the state—our local governments included—do not on the whole actually serve us. Whatever benefits we get tend to be incidental and always under threat. However, we might not go as far as saying we are living our lives in conflict with the state. And yet, in some of our experiences helping out friends and neighbors, we may have actually come into direct conflict with the state, or its enforcement in the form of police. We are told we can't do something that seems totally normal, even unquestionably necessary. The most glaring examples of course come in righteous spontaneous protest—in the USA often in response to police murder of Black people, though also importantly in Indigenous-led protection of land from extraction—where regular people without "political" experience directly face the brute force of the state in the form of rubber bullets, tear gas, beatdowns, and arrest. The state will object to even simple kindness or humane treatment if it isn't concentrated through its own power. For example, most cities have an ongoing war against their unhoused populations and will actively terrorize both those living outside or seeking shelter and people in the community who consider them neighbors worthy of mutual aid.

Our bitter conflict with the state isn't always as explicit as all that. It goes deeper, layered into our histories. One helpful story can be seen in the food we eat. In *A Mess of Greens: Southern Gender and Southern*

Food, Elizabeth S. D. Engelhardt shows how in the southern United States, an intentional effort was taken, alongside driving people off subsistence farming in rural communities towards waged jobs in factory towns, to rethink working people's diet. Instead of skillet cornbread, for example—something a subsistence farming family could produce on its own—it was deemed more "nutritional" (the backing of medicine and science) to eat wheat-based breads. Through the invention of home economics, white women with meager means were driven away from the traditional foodways that fitted living in conjunction with the land towards the need to purchase new cooking utensils and foods. Thus, we have white bread as a staple. Versions of this class-based, racialized, or ethnic degradation of local foodways can be found all over the world, especially as consumer culture monotonizes the available products for us to eat—and as more people come to live in food deserts where the only available shopping is at a poorly stocked gas station mart.

In other words, regardless of whether we realize that we are in open conflict with the state, the state is constantly waging war on us, particularly any form of autonomous power that isn't mediated through state bureaucracy—the gentler side, as the decolonial revolutionary Frantz Fanon argues in *The Wretched of the Earth*, of the police power that beats people into submission. Doing politics in the authorized way—voting, mostly, but also petitions and sanctioned protests—clearly makes little difference to the mass of people around the globe, since it encloses us in very narrow definitions of action while also removing our connection from the people, living creatures, and world around us by imagining policy and state infrastructure as the only means for managing life. While a vision of freedom from the stranglehold of the state often includes fantasies of violent confrontation or guerrilla warfare, this book focuses instead on how to divert the energy of engaging directly with the state towards rethinking approaches to life. This approach can be seen as the underpinnings of counterpower—the idea that we can build liberated structures in the spaces left open or abandoned by the state. It's not merely an idea: it's both a fact and long-standing tactic of survival that mirrors the history of the development of the state. One important model is marronage, the communities of Black people who freed themselves from slavery, took up living in unused land alongside Indigenous people and traitorous Europeans, and performed raids and liberations on the slaveocracy.

Anarchism as a Countertheory of Power

There is a saying in certain marginalized communities, "my existence is resistance," which epitomizes how racialized groups, as well as gendered/sexualized people, are put into a position of inherent opposition to the state and its power plays. (And I need to note that our understanding of gender is always racialized as a continuous historical production of colonialism.) In *As Black as Resistance*, Zoé Samudzi and William C. Anderson theorize that Blackness in the USA exists outside the supposed benefits of the state and the sanctioned norms of citizenship, being violently excluded on institutional and material levels. However, they argue, this position still requires an extra step to become part of a struggle for liberation, especially in attempts to avoid being captured by the logics of the state. Yet, people who inhabit the various, overlapping identity positions specially targeted for exclusion and violence may also just wish to live their lives: "It's just my life, it's not political. Not everything I do as a Black person, as a transwoman, as a Black transwoman, and so on, is an explicit or implicit conflict with the state. Sometimes, I just need to survive."

I feel an affinity with both sides of this idea, appreciating that certain forms of existence are criminalized, made illegal, targeted, and therefore become sites of articulating resistance; and that existing within these spaces doesn't always have to be "political," it's just living. In a way, my approach to anarchism attempts to do justice to both these feelings—the desire to survive and the desire for freedom both represent a desire to live. The articulation of anarchism given in this book argues that these desires aren't mutually exclusive. Direct resistance and just living form a whole in terms of how our lives extend beyond the reach of the state, no matter how much the state tries to encroach on every aspect of our lives, to interject itself into every relationship, to become the arbiter of every problem and decision.

Many of the ways that people are "just living" already enact transformative approaches to life from the point of view of statecraft. For example, the ways that people within various targeted communities, like Black queer social groups or many Indigenous cultures, resolve conflict outside of police and courts, both because the institutions subject them to violence and because they have cultural practices that predate or counter colonialism. Other common examples include queer ways of doing kinship, sharing of labor and care work—especially childcare—and the unquestioning sharing of resources, which run contrary to capitalist norms that depict us as being in competition with everyone else, and thus force us to grasp tightly to what little we have in our tiny family blocs.

There is an argument to be made against turning these living scraps of freedom, where I locate anarchism, into an explicit political theory. If the process of state/market hegemony that has produced racial, gender, sexual, and labor oppression has been able to take over all the elements of life that it comes across, maybe we need to keep some things out of the light to avoid capture. So often, for example, grassroots mutual aid efforts in the wake of weather disasters get co-opted by the state. But anarchism avoids prescription, and as we discuss later, the act of representation of these moments of freedom risks turning the fleeting possibility into an eternal claim. Instead of blueprints, anarchist writing often uses the examples of historical stateless people, or of the remaining resistant lifeways under colonialism to describe life that could be, and in fact already is, otherwise. Similarly, in radical science fiction, these alternatives are often imagined and constructed in forms that provide practical inspiration for changing our daily patterns.

Anarchist-influenced theory can still serve a purpose without succumbing to prescription or capture, especially as a way to help us find each other in our desires for freedom. These invisible zones of freedom—what I want to call "no place"— fuel resistance merely by making our lives full and textured amid the alienation of the neoliberal world order, and help us improvise direct action in truly revolutionary moments. These spaces, non-places, have theoretical potential, as long as we don't see theory as a framework for practice and action but rather a reflection on what we do each day, the kinds of creatures we are, that holds in its line of sight collective liberation, showing us how we can start from here, right now.

A practical, flexible anarchism works on the microscopic scale, as a part of intentionality in all of our daily actions, from our way of treating ourselves, to our friends and surroundings, our community and environment. If anarchism is understood in opposition to all forms of hierarchy, power, and control, and in favor of collective freedom, then we can gauge each of our actions from the perspective of how it contributes towards the larger project of collective freedom, understanding always that our pathways to liberation are necessarily tied into others, and that all forms of oppression are harmful to all groups, though the level of harm varies. This process-oriented idea of anarchism includes within it an expectation of failure and acknowledgment, and attempts to try better. But our failure is also part of our refusal to give ourselves to a system out to kill us all. It's not perfect, there's no end goal, but it can lead to releasing us from unnecessary feelings of duty to abstract ideas of nation or identity, while strengthening our bonds to the people and world around us.

The argument of this book, then, is that we are always already doing anarchy in all the moments and spaces that aren't taken over by market and state. Within us, we contain a sanctioned identity, not only in terms of race, gender, and sexuality, but also in the idea of a selfsame individual who is responsible for their own survival through the accumulation of money and property. But that sanctioned aspect of who we are doesn't exhaust our (embodied and desiring) experience, which is much more grounded in our connection to others around us. In fact, we live mostly there, in the no place that provides some refuge from the surveilling eyes of power. For the end of these forms of oppression to come, there have to remain spaces of resistance, like, for example, the Zapatista-controlled areas in Chiapas, or the defended spaces of Rojava amid the Syrian war, and ongoing lifeways of Indigenous groups all over the world that have not been destroyed by the joined forces of state and capital. It's not that "nature abhors a vacuum"; rather, the world can only persist with wastelands that evade productive use. It's capitalism and the state, the drive for profit and property, that cannot withstand unused, unnamed spaces.

There are occupations, temporary autonomous zones, moments, and spaces of solidarity and joining that undo the structures of power— if only temporarily from the point of view of linear time, though I argue later that these fleeting moments are indeed the freedom we aim for, and these spaces escape the colonial mapping of total extraction. These times and spaces are the foundations for resistance. The history of state and capital has always sparked fierce resistance even as those stories are erased. But the end of the genocidal domination of Euro-American colonialism can only be imagined if the workers inside of their domains find ways to betray the demands of state and market. And so this book wants to locate the places and moments where we are doing that, creating networks of care and support, the kind of labor that gets overlooked and erased (and is largely feminized and racialized), and yet it is this work that makes life possible and provides space for joy and resistance.

Therefore, this book won't tell you the best strategies or tactics to bring on the revolution, nor will it be a retelling of anarchistic histories. Its aim isn't to seize the state and wield it dubiously towards the people's freedom (spoiler alert: that never works). Neither will it operate in the liberal manner of guilting and shaming you into noting your complicity with the horrors of the world and thus imagining the solution is in your wallet or reducing your carbon footprint (thus letting the state off the hook). Though it's true that we are all complicit to the extent that we inhabit this shared world, we also have varying degrees of complicity—acknowledging this enables us to betray the questionable benefits of citizenship or belonging to a nation, and repurpose our access to resources against the hierarchies of power that frame our world. In fact, we can shift the fact of our complicity in this world order to a different terrain and translate "complicity" instead to mean that we have our survival bound up with each other. Thus, this book is going to locate sources of liberation in our relationships, in transformative approaches to relating to each other, all life, the world itself.

How to End Things

One of the main refrains of this book is that things don't need to last forever. Thus, a theory of freedom means ending, moving on, letting go, and letting be. The biggest insight of anarchism might lie in dissolution. The flexibility that uses temporary structures to get things done, and then dissolves those structures before power and control settle in. This tilting towards dissolution is essential to an anti-state position. The state postures as a forever institution that organizes our lives totally, just as capitalism has been theorized as the inescapable end of history. Against this totalizing pretension, people often remind us that the state is a relatively recent invention and capitalism a fairly recent development, just as the carceral system of prisons and policing are also recent blights on our world. An anarchist point of view doesn't seek to replace these institutions with better permanent structures, which might only trap us yet again.

Let's think of anarchism as a form of breaking up. Break up with your lover, your friends, your family, your job, your presuppositions! Only in the break can you reimagine the right boundaries that allow you to engage with all of these types of relationships out of a position of autonomy and mutual care. Anarchism operates through the ability to end things (relationships, groups, institutions, states) that don't work. If anarchism opposes hierarchy, then it needs to be cautious in adhering to any space where it may become static, controlling, or corrupt. But even on a much simpler level, we can see it as a practical admission that not everything works forever, and therefore we need to always be open to moving on and trying something new.

Let's flip the state on its head and apply the theory of break-ups to this ultimate claim of stability. Many critical analyses of the distribution of power and control within nation states points to how the normalized identity of the citizen is dependent on subordinate and oppressed groups. Within a capitalist, racist, patriarchal, colonial system, this means that the poor, the racialized, the people who don't conform to gender and sexual norms, can be treated as disposable. If entire swaths of the population are disposable, then why not dispose of the state? The various global nations' response to the Covid-19 pandemic has made it even clearer how little value our lives have in relation to keeping the economic wheels turning. From lockdowns that imposed unevenly distributed restrictions on people, to the insistence that certain workers perform their jobs in unsafe conditions, to the utter lack of health infrastructure and economic support to help people survive during this moment, states have clearly failed us. What little they gave to the people they govern is a pittance compared to the money that continues to be funneled into big businesses, militaries, and the police.

In the space of need that was created, mutual aid groups flourished everywhere, not simply out of necessity but because they were the best method of getting things people needed to the people who needed them. In my local area, our mutual aid group already had roots due to responses to climate catastrophes like devastating hurricanes and floods. The connections were in place and revamped for the particular needs apparent during Covid-19. But this goes to show that with capitalist-driven ecological destruction wreaking havoc on us, the people with the least, who are less ensconced in the systems that hold them in place, are the most able to respond flexibly to problems with fixes and solutions.

Mutual aid was initially theorized by the early anarchist Peter Kropotkin, drawing of the practices of animals and people, and has continued to be a running theme in much of anarchist literature, where, for example, Colin Ward calls his *Anarchy in Action* an "extended footnote" to Kropotkin's book. All the arguments about mutual aid point to its spontaneity as a form of organizing in the face of need. We don't need a theory of mutual aid—it's what we do. However, anarchists will also see mutual aid as a place for radicalization, to bring people into the idea that we can share resources without the state intervening. In *The Nation on No Map*, William C. Anderson warns that when we provide the means of survival in the absence of the state, without confronting the state, these forms can either help relegitimate that state or risk co-optation and integration into the state's own institutional framework. Without the politicized aspect, they operate like charities, which prop up uneven distribution of resources. It's most important to see it against the prevalent idea of charity, which keeps the hierarchies of have and have not intact. Mutual aid is a kind of circulation within community, horizontally, that can operate outside the dictates of a market or hierarchies of labor. If Ward equates his concept of anarchism with mutual aid, we can thus see it not simply as a spontaneous and effective form of organizing lives—something that is natural to many creatures in the world, despite the survival of the fittest narrative that misreadings of evolutionary theory ascribe to all life. Mutual aid is also a call to action—a way of recreating our lives in connection with others.

Anarchism shows that these situations work due to their flexibility. A hierarchical organization has to receive top-down orders before anyone can act. Anarchist organizing works through horizontal dynamics and emphasizes direct action (though it too can get mired in processes that avoid decisions and accountability). These two principles mean that there isn't a leader to defer to for decision making, but in contrast to how bureaucracy abdicates responsibility, the anarchist version of decentralizing empowers each person or group to do what they need without asking for permission. This can lead to problems, mistakes, and failures—but they are embedded within a community that has outlined a common aim of liberation rather than the eternal mistakes of the state for which no one will ever be accountable. The community can reflect and critique and then reorient for the next problem.

The anarchist organizing principle of the affinity group, which is typically traced to nineteenth-century Spain, is helpful here. As opposed to parties and hierarchies of leadership and committees, the affinity group brings together like-minded people for a collaborative project, whether a form of direct action or community work. The group itself has no intention of lasting beyond the purpose that brought it together. If operating on the basis of consensus, where group decisions need the consent of each member, then a person who disagrees can decide to leave the group if it takes a direction they no longer agree with. The larger organizational method this implies is something like a loose network of groups forming and unforming and coordinating to get things done. Not only does the affinity group allow for a flexible organizing that is project oriented, it avoids the concentration of power that bureaucracies and state infrastructure tend to impose. The affinity group is made to break up.

The commonly cited pitfall of this kind of organizing method, much caricaturized during the Occupy movements, is that a consensus-based process, where a decision or action can only be made when everyone agrees, can take a long time or even involve an endless blocking by one person objecting repeatedly. However, this is where the idea of affinity and dissolution comes in. If one person keeps blocking, then they would need to think about what they are doing in the group. Perhaps they have a different view of how things should be and rather than hold up the group, the group should reform without them, and they can form their own group. Basing our actions and decisions on affinity allows for a supple process of working together—and knowing when not to work together. Instead of the fear of the tyranny of the majority (or minority) that attends the discourse of democracy, it looks realistically at the fact that not everyone will agree, but no one person's or group's decision should alter everyone's life (and especially not forever).

In the following chapters of this book, I explore in more detail how approaching our relationships to each other, to jobs and work, to land and property, to institutions and the state, in this manner can add up to a radical change in life. If we operate from a principle of autonomy, which doesn't mean my autonomy over yours but mutual autonomy, then we can see more clearly where our capabilities lie, what our limitations are, and what we can accomplish working together. Ultimately, I want this book to show how the stringing along of these little moments of anarchy in our daily lives helps to weave a revolution that would allow us to disidentify with the larger power structures in our life, from the identities we are given to the power of control over us. Of course, conceiving of this as simply an individualized endeavor isn't going to accomplish a large-scale revolution that overthrows that state and capital, but it can prepare the way by showing us that we don't have to fear what comes after. One of the major ways the state and market retain control is by instilling the fear in us that whatever else is out there is worse. And as this approach to anarchism is relational, it is something that we will practice in community, transforming the foundations of our world, so that we no longer reproduce power but something else.

No, this isn't simply an individualist approach, though it is grounded in shifting internal perspectives. Our individual disidentification opens us up to larger networks of care and community that we can then build the world from. This relation between our own personal delinking and the building of community is what many anarchists would call prefiguration: our actions create the world we want right now, we don't have to wait for the revolution to start another, better world. The introductory anarchist zine *Life without Law* defines prefiguration, as well as direct action, through the idea that "we find the means and the ends to be inseparable." Anarchists argue that the means of our struggle can't betray the principles of the ends we are struggling for. This distinction is what has historically differentiated anarchists from (authoritarian) communists (going back to the much discussed split in the First International)—many Marxists believe that we can use the state to achieve liberation.

The state isn't going to wither away. This fact is shown by the failed communist revolutions, which ended up reproducing authoritarian states. Likewise, the argument of this book isn't that if everyone simply injects their lives with these principles of anarchism, we will magically reach an anarchist utopia. Still, an important factor of change is to undo the working of authority in our head and in our enacted relationships with others. In our limited lives, we come to see the shape of the world as predictable and eternal. And yet everything we've inherited as the seeming immutable contours of our lives is of a fairly recent origin, compared to the amount of time people have been living on this planet—and anyway, it all happens to be crumbling right before our eyes. In fact, the process of normalization and adaptation is arguably one of the reasons why the ongoing climate catastrophe gets increasingly dire and the possible responses fewer: we've normalized inaction. Even the most radical leftist will reproduce state thinking in their lives, because it takes a continual vigilance for us not to internalize and repeat the logic of the state. This book therefore serves as an accessible, practical set of guidelines as to how we might dislodge the state from its perch when it comes to engaging with each other and our lives, with the hope that this allows more room to glimpse what in our lives is already a source of our freedom, and so collectivize it and push for more. If all of our lives have been rendered surplus by the tag team of state and market, then we might as well just take what we want.

We want it all.

FAQs

Isn't anarchy just chaos and violence? How can I see it in my life?

For our purposes, we can break down the practice of anarchism into two interconnected categories. The first, which gets the most (negative) attention, is direct action, insurrection, and revolutionary confrontation with the state and its institutions—in other words, actions people take to demolish the society we live in based on racism, misogyny, capitalism, borders, homophobia, etc., to clear the way for a better world based on interdependency and self-determination. The better world is the purview of the second category: the relationships we form through care and connection, which give the lie to the structures of hierarchy imposed on us through family, education, church, work, and other institutions. In this book, we are focusing on the way anarchism actually infuses our lives right now, and how we can amplify its effects. Whenever we join together to solve problems, to help take care of each other, to promote well-being and autonomy, we are enacting anarchist ideas of spontaneous organizing without control.

Isn't anarchism just impossible?

By painting anarchism as chaotic and violent, the dominant thought makes it seem distasteful. When we contend more directly with the "utopian" visions of anarchism—a world of shared freedom and responsibility—it's a bigger threat to the colonial world order we inhabit. So much work goes into making us believe it is impossible by making all facets of a society of control, of borders and nations and states and capital, seem inevitable: the outcome of progress, civilization, and development. But when we shift our focus onto the way we actually live, when we don't identify with the power structures that rule us, we can see that anarchism already exists in practice and we can rebuild the world through prioritizing these different social relationships over the motives of capitalism and state-sanctioned identities.

2

Are Relationships Even Possible?
Anarchy at Home

I am saying that the ultimate connection cannot be the enemy. The ultimate connection must be the need that we find between us. It is not only who you are, in other words, but what we can do for each other that will determine the connection.

June Jordan, "Report from the Bahamas"

- Learning boundaries
- How to break up
- Relationships without hierarchy
- Experimenting and failing

Denaturalizing Hieararchy in Our Lives

Our thinking has become so aligned with the presumed static quality of the state—the inevitability of government and capitalism—that we seek things that will last forever. In relationships, we feel this most strongly when we fall in love. But even that moment is telling: the intensity of falling in love is necessarily momentary, yet it has promises of forever. If that relationship develops, it has to change, and thus the question of forever becomes a different question of growth and change, which needs to face the possibility of breaking up. Permanence seems to give some kind of comfort, even to the extent of forgiving some "necessary evils," whether in the bad behavior of a partner or the "bad apple" argument about murderous police. Yet, in our lifetime, we've seen the end of marriage as a seemingly eternal institution, just as we've seen the nuclear hetero family, while still imposed as an ideal, become less frequently realized in practice, with single parents, co-parenting after divorce, blended families, and informal networks of care that allow for people to work and raise children against all odds.

On an interpersonal level, we can see how our relationships with other people play out. Besides the overbearing claim to eternity of the nuclear family—which masks forms of discipline, control, and false claims of unconditional love—there is freedom in leaving behind relationships, not even always acrimoniously. Maybe they worked for a time. Maybe they reached their limit. Maybe they were situational: I had these friends as a child because there were not many other options for a kid who didn't have freedom of movement. I lived in a certain city for a few years. When it became possible to meet other people or move somewhere else, I left those friends behind and made others—who also worked for me for a time, until I made more changes.

We are often bound to imagine our singular choices as eternal choices: professional careers, to the extent that any of us are still able to grab hold of one these days, are seen as vocations. Even our purchasing is seen as somehow embodying our identity: we are what we buy. There's an old adage about a person being made up by their actions, but once we assume our identities to be these unchangeable natural essences, we become confined to these roles. This assignment of identity isn't merely a consumer choice, or even a style or aesthetic, though it encompasses it. It arguably extends to the other social-political-economic positions we are made to take up like race, gender, sexuality, and class (which impinge on culture, or rather are produced by the social relations we inhabit). Of course, not all of these things can simply be left behind, especially as the dynamics of power work by naturalizing these positions, so that race is seemingly evident by skin color and gender is seemingly evident by genitals, so-called secondary sexual traits, or genetic material. However, all identity formations function as disciplinary traps, just as much as they can enable us to find like-minded people among a sea of strangers.

The anarchist argument, which aligns with the feminist slogan that the personal is political, points out that the way we relate to others is another place to root out power over others, discipline, and hierarchy. The kinds of relationships we uphold regulate our acceptance into normal society. Deviations can be punished, ranging from lack of opportunity to outright violence. But even before we get into the aspects of gender and sexuality more explicitly, we can simply investigate our relationships through the lens of power, hierarchy, and constraint—or on the other side, mutuality, equality, and autonomy. Relationships—particularly cisheterosexual ones—often get framed as power struggles, but we can live them differently, outside of the idea of scarcity of love.

Our Relationships and the State

Part of the process of normalizing capitalism as a mode of life—which has been an ongoing and violent process of removing people's impulses for collaboration and ability to sustain themselves outside the state—has been to instill competition as the evolutionary truth about how all creatures live. We compete for resources. The biggest, strongest, and smartest survives. There even exist whole tracks of scientific study done to "prove" that the inhuman traits that capitalism rewards for the few are actually innate human tendencies. Sure, we might agree that there is a survival instinct (which all animals ostensibly share). However, survival tends to work best collectively, not individually as a competition for resource and spaces. As I mentioned, this fact is the basis of Kropotkin's claim in *Mutual Aid*, which turns the social Darwinist or eugenicist thinking on its head to give a different picture of collaboration, evolution, and co-survival. And Kropotkin was only recording what many stateless groups had been doing throughout history.

Capitalism tries to naturalize the idea that survival is best pursued through self-interest, which in a situation of (imposed) scarcity necessarily comes at the cost of others' survival. It is only one tiny step from there to the imposition of racial hierarchies, which further entrench the gendered and sexual hierarchies, determining who naturally deserves more and who deserves less. The Hobbesian idea of society as a war of all against all sets the table for the notion that the state will protect us from potential aggressors. The state, via the media, uses this discourse of violence alongside promises of security to delegitimate collective action and legitimate its own force and control. However, this presumed protection given to us by the state actually cloaks the fact that the state is continually waging war on us—to varying degrees, depending on our different positions within racialized class systems. The same protective impulse the state plays up becomes the paternalistic care that the man of the house extends to the women and children in his life, so that the household becomes a mini-state. This paternalistic alibi excuses extension of power, for example, in terms of anti-LGBT policies, such as the infamous bathroom bills, under the cover of protecting women and girls. Much repressive policy operates with the notion of protecting children.

The normalization of hierarchy starts right away in our lives, with adults ruling over children (or minors, as the state defines them). In the patriarchal bourgeois family, imposed as the norm over the last couple of hundred years of colonial conquest and industrial development, the father reigns over the mother and the children. This model in the family merely reflects the father's experience at work, where a boss rules over him. The chain of hierarchy goes up to the state, where the president looks over his citizens like a stern father. The extension of the nuclear family as an expectation of social arrangement for all classes and races has an uneven history, and today it's questionable to what extent anyone actually experiences anything like this ideal. But still, for most, the family is the fallback position of care and dependency, and in the primacy of parental rights it replicates forms of control. This form of social organization not only took over more communal living arrangements for the European peasantry, it also erased the histories of different forms of kinship that Indigenous people practiced in the Americas and in Africa, as well as other colonized territories. The model was later imposed on descendants of these groups—in the USA, specifically to hold up racist ideologies of blood quantum and Blackness—as a value from which to judge an excluded group's inability to assimilate. The replacement of extended kinship structures with nuclear families severs networks of care that everyone needs to survive, and ties us into the eternal bonds of blood belonging that often feel inescapable and harmful.

The work of Nigerian gender scholar Oyèrónké Oyěwùmí explains how hierarchy is so ingrained in Western colonial culture that we imagine people's identities to preexist the social relations they live within, as if we are simply plugged fully formed into an already operational society. Oyěwùmí ascribes this to the privileging of the sense of sight in Western culture, which helps naturalize differences and hierarchies: race and gender are seen on the body and then used to classify people along the social hierarchy of racism and misogyny. When things are as plain as sight, we deny the possibility of understanding how social relations are actually constantly producing these systems of power in every interaction. In precolonial Yoruba culture, Oyěwùmí explains, people's words and interactions determined their social position. This truth underlies our colonial world as well. If we are what we do, rather than what we are perceived to be, this might then give us the power to undo these hierarchies by reframing all of our interactions with the people, other creatures, and life around us as world-creating. It may be a long process of disidentification, but this is the internal and collective work that forms a part of transforming the world.

Starting with children, we might view the relationship between parent and child not as one of domination, property, or discipline, but rather one of support and care. Human babies are famously born "prematurely," in that they need constant care for an extended period of time after birth in order to survive. Many parents will confess that early childcare tends to feel mostly like becoming a vessel to serve the needs of the child (which if you think about it undoes the apparent hierarchy of parents over children). As the child gains more control over their movement, and thus relative independence, we can try to think about our relation of care to them through anarchist ideas. One of the initial myths we have to destroy is the sense of ownership over a child. If you biologically reproduce, you might be able to attest to the fact that a new baby is a totally new person whom you have to meet and get to know. To non-biological parents, this is quite obvious. Blood belonging becomes a coercive form of control, and the subtle words of parenting do so much to discipline children into limiting their horizons to the expectations of the parents.

The strongest role of a caregiver ends up being a baseline support for autonomous exploration and self-development—this is the basic idea of the psychoanalyst D. W. Winnicott's concept of the "good enough" mother. The drive to be a good parent usually overshoots the mark, confining the child, while abandonment or lack of interest is also clearly harmful. The good enough mother is there but not hovering, not interfering. It's hard not to run around saying "no" to all the potential crises your mind can multiply when watching a toddling child navigate their world, but parents can try to instill a sense of autonomy in their children. The partner with whom I co-parent a child showed me that you must question each time you want to say "no" to see whether you are merely trying to limit your own trouble (to make your life easier or more convenient) or truly keeping the child from harm. Many of the "no's" caregivers give to children have to do with their own comfort and are thus arbitrary boundaries the child comes up against.

Boundaries, or If You Love Someone, Set Them Free

And yet, boundaries are necessary to protect our individual autonomy and enable collective care. Contrary to what one might expect from an anarchist, I am going to propose that understanding boundaries are the essential thing we can learn from an anarchist approach to maintaining (and ending) relationships. I say this with a little bit of irony, given that anarchists are consistently critical of the false boundaries created by the borders of the nation state (and likewise of the seemingly essential borderlines of state-sanctioned identity like gender, race, and class). At a certain point, when I started spending my time mostly among other anarchist-inclined people, I also started feeling more empowered to say "no" to things. One feeling that make me feel pressured into committing myself to situations, events, and spaces that I actually didn't want to participate in was my own sense of needing to do things, of not missing out, of fear of being alone or boredom. In the world of organizing, this feeling compels people to overwork themselves, therefore replicating the capitalist emphasis on perpetual productivity. Another feeling causing me to say "yes" when I didn't want to was (an ultimately imagined) sense of others' expectations of me. It became much clearer to navigate saying "no" with a group of people who could revise expectations based on a person's clear communication of needs and boundaries, that is, my anarchist friends. We shared a mutual understanding that our needs are changing, and even when we want to be with others, sometimes we need to be alone. Of course, skipping on engagements doesn't help you when you feel like you are missing out. But I began to experience a deeper sense of my need for downtime and being alone, and realized that my overcommitment actually caused its own loss of solitude.

Prentis Hemphill's essay "Boundaries Can Be Love," in adrienne maree brown's book, *Holding Change*, shows that boundaries are "the distance at which I could love me and you simultaneously." As opposed to the walls we build in response to trauma, which "reinforce or create a static worldview that is transferable to other conditions, other relationships," Hemphill claims that boundaries are "responsive, movable, and highly dependent on real-time assessments." The imagery of static as opposed to movable is helpful here for framing an anarchist approach to relationships. Just as anarchism wants to dissolve the eternal and totalizing claims of capitalism and the state, it proposes a mobile, changing, transformative understanding of how we relate to one another. In this mode, boundaries create opportunities for genuine connection, rather than defensively shutting out one another. Of course, the ability to set up boundaries and observe them takes practice. We are usually expected by our family, our loved ones, our work, to be always available, to take on more work at the expense of our own ability to subsist or survive, to take on any emotional trouble by the people we support. Once you start practicing boundaries, as Hemphill writes, you start to realize what things you actually want to do, how long you can stay present to a situation, what relationships feel healthy and nourishing, and which are draining or even abusive. Furthermore, you can be more in touch with your own need for care and support and find a voice to ask for it. A necessary distance allows for us to see each other and communicate—as opposed to the selfless merger so often modeled through family and normative relationships. It allows for a measurement of ability, energy, space, and even the gaps in time we need to hear and understand each other.

The space between us can give us the grounds for saying no. And in a way, anarchism as a daily practice can be seen as an accumulation of refusals. Saying no may not in itself amount to a revolution, but linking our no's together is an important part of living our lives today as we hope to live them in the future. Practicing saying no to the minimal things we don't want to do can also help us build towards bigger refusals: against work, against money, against our neoliberal identities. An anarchist approach to relating with friends, community, and others, then, prioritizes clear communication about needs, desires, and wishes, and also a respect for the refusal of others to meet those needs, desires, and wishes based on their capacity. Disabled communities use "spoon theory" to discuss capacity from moment to moment. Each person has a limited number of spoons, and each task—even the most minimal—takes up a spoon. When one is out of spoons, one no longer has space for more. To enumerate one's capacity as a changing thing day to day allows one to rethink commitments and needs. Of course, this innovation comes from the experiences of people who cannot and will not meet the demands of an ableist culture based on constant production. Hearing "no" can move from respect for a child's autonomy, to the understanding of a lack of interest or desire in intimacy, to the refusal to offer free or even paid labor. The communication must be mutual, and like with affinity groups for organizing purposes, an alignment of needs, wishes, and desires can lead to exciting interactions. Meanwhile, a recognition of a misalignment can lead to a thrilling release of unnecessary connections. In other words, we have to let our own expectations of others go in order to be able to have non-coercive relationships.

Many people experience the first burst of falling in love with someone that comes with a revelation of shared interests, mutual attraction, and intense dedication of time (which is often stolen from other obligations like work). The follow-up to these moments can often be a realization of incompatibility. That is, if you haven't fallen into some kind of relationship structure or cling to another person out of fear of loneliness. I'm not saying that the initial burst of love or infatuation doesn't have its own benefit—it's one of the pleasures of life, and it reminds us that we aren't simply productivity machines. But the lesson of the dying of the spark is also worth learning: a momentary alignment of interests and desire is not a promise of a continuing relationship, so we can remove the expectations that anything ought to last. Just like we are taught that institutions that supposedly serve us are eternal and unchanging, we tend to model our relationships on an idea of longevity (or even eternity). People have their childhood best friends that they cart along with them into adulthood, even if they turn out to be totally at odds with each other (or if your childhood friend was actually a bully—it often takes years to realize that your "best friend" may have contributed immensely to internalized feelings of shame and incompetence). Many of our early relationships are ultimately coercive to the extent that we don't get to choose our surroundings.

One of the trickiest things to be able to do in a relationship that spans a long chunk of our lifetime is to be able to reflect mutually on growth and change in the other. This situation is equally true of caring for children as it is for attempting intimate partnership. It's a matter of letting the other person transform outside of whatever expectations you project on them, and delighting in this change. This problem comes up so clearly in family dynamics, where families create stories for each member— usually a typical anecdote that stands in for a person's entire personality. These stories are almost impossible to escape, creating the feeling of being sucked into performing that character any time we enter a family space. A relationship built on mutual respect for autonomy would allow for the other person to be different one day to the next. This possibility of change also comes with the risk of losing closeness and connection. And so, fundamentally, we need to rethink our relationships as creating their own timelines, their own rhythms, and their own ends.

Consent and Its Limits

Much of anarchist discourse on relationships, particularly sexual ones, focuses on the idea of consent. This discourse has reached some parts of the mainstream through "consent culture," which is seemingly opposed to "rape culture." The basic premise is that from the time we are young we are denied bodily autonomy. The care given to an infant quickly pushes over into the torture of pinched cheeks, forced hugs, and painful tickles. Framing touch and intimacy through the ability to consent to any interaction aims to regain the autonomy we are trained out of. One model of consent is that in touch, whether friendly or more intimate, one asks for the verbal affirmation that the touch is desired: asking before hugging or kissing. This model replaces the "no means no," used by certain feminist movements to define rape, with "yes means yes"—in other words, even if "no" isn't said, if "yes" isn't said also, then the touch may be veering into unwanted territory.

In a patriarchal society, the absence of bodily autonomy ends up getting normalized for feminized people, perhaps first through the cat-and-mouse game of teenage straight courtship, where a boy builds a girl up and then wears her down until she gives him the sex he desires. Later, it comes through the expectation to continue serving men through sex, whether this is in marriage, other defined relationships, or in sex work. And the culmination of this absence of autonomy is in the expectation to reproduce, to conceive, bear, and raise children. Already we can see that the very idea of consent is hard to pin down, since the normalized relationships consist of winning over a hesitant partner. A person may say "yes" and mean "no," or realize they didn't want something to happen afterwards, or feel unsafe to fully articulate their feelings. Furthermore, a situation can start with a "yes" and change to a "no" at any point. For these reasons, a simple understanding of consent won't work. One framework is the idea of non-coercive consent, which reminds us that we can consent through coercion, and therefore not mean "yes." We have to dig deeper into the way we relate, in order to create space to hold complexity, difficult communication, confusion, and change.

Sex is so hard to navigate because our gender and our sexuality are entirely wrapped up in our sense of our identities. We are told we need to discover who we are, a singular identity that demands us to be one thing and not another—or many other things at different times and places. And yet we have multiple and conflicting desires that are entangled in our sense of ourselves, and this connects with how we want to be seen, touched, and spoken to, and who we want to see, touch, and speak with, and these desires shift over time. In our relationships we might still prefigure other ways of being, whether it's a matter of decontextualizing the forms of hierarchy and oppression through mimicry (which some kinks might do), or loosening our claims on others and ourselves, loosening our grips on the ideas of what relationships need to look like, and enjoying the momentary pleasures of being together. Giving ourselves permission for our desires can help us encounter others with less shame, less feeling of a need to control, and more awareness of the ways the stories we tell about ourselves overlap the endless physical combinations our bodies can create to form bonds of love, care, and sex.

The introductory anarchist zine, *Life without Law*, connects consent to the anarchist mode of organizing called consensus, drawing connections between one-on-one encounters and group dynamics. For a group operating on consensus, the idea is that everyone must agree, or consent, to the action that the group will take collectively. In a full consensus process, if anyone blocks the action, then the group must either drop the action or continue discussion until they reach consensus. From this angle, we might shift emphasis from consent or consensus, towards dissent and dissolution: anarchism as breaking up. If we translate this into the realm of physical and emotional intimacy, the process of consent becomes one of being able to withdraw at any moment—and also knowing that that process isn't always clear in the moment.

We must then relate to consent as an imperfect tool to help us navigate the world as it currently exists, where so often people's bodily autonomy, as well as time and labor, are not respected. It doesn't give us a strict set of rules to follow, and it also doesn't mean that every intimate encounter is rife with danger (cis straight men have complained that the idea of consent makes them afraid of being accused of being a rapist). In a way, it fits the grid of anarchism we are developing, as a way to gauge our interactions and promote mutual autonomy in every interaction. Perhaps we can boil down the idea of consent simply to no one owes you physical intimacy, or even love, no matter what has been said or done before within a relationship, rather than getting stuck in the contractual model of receiving consent from a partner for each moment of touch. And if we keep in mind that people's feelings and capacities change, that all emotions are things we move through, we can take a step back from the intensity to understand that no affirmation or denial of consent (or love or affection) is necessarily eternal. It would be much better to listen and to be attentive to all the cues that people send us in our relationships—and also to be open to accepting accountability even for an unintentional harm. If we think of relationships as ever changing, veering towards dissolution, we prepare ourselves to let go rather than to grasp when we don't get what we (think we) want.

The idea of consent is important, particularly for creating boundaries and temporary bridges across them to facilitate our relationships. Yet, consent isn't liberatory. As C. E. argues in "Undoing Sex," it presumes we know what we want, it presumes us to have stable identities that never change, it presumes that sex isn't somehow linked to violence and trauma and that good sex is possible. And when we strictly adhere to the consent model, we have to infinitesimally receive consent over the course of a series of touches, because people can quickly go from a sense of enjoyment to a sense of violation without warning. And even more importantly, the experience of violation often can't be said in the moment, as trauma can force silence—or may only be realized after the fact.

Ultimately, imagining liberated sexuality is another situation where we would have to take a leap into the unknown outside of the social relations we are steeped in currently, or else we run the risk of merely reversing the seeming dynamics of oppression. Going back to the claim from *Wages against Housework*, it is only outside of the relationships that we are forced to uphold through capitalism that we can even begin to know what our sexuality might be, or what love would feel like. We still live in a rape culture, where accountability for violation is almost never reached, and where certain people are held outside even the basic recognition of their bodily autonomy due to racism and colonialism. "Good" sex is entangled with the idea of coercive sex, if only as a way to imagine something that isn't violent. Perhaps in the end we can just relieve ourselves from the attempt to work out our identity through sex and put it in its place.

Multiply Our Models of Relationship

Just as countless societies for untold generations have organized themselves by means and structures that do not conform to the current norm of the state, the market, or other forms of institutional governance, relationships have been practiced along any number of different lines than exclusive heterosexual dedication in a couple, the enclosed nuclear family based on genetic belonging, or the subordination of friends and collectives of care to one's blood ties—or even the distinction between "real" family and an extended community. In the "modern" context, the classical anarchists of the nineteenth and early twentieth centuries were often proponents of various versions of "free love" and relationships outside of marriage or coupling. Anarchists weren't the only ones pointing to other forms of relationship—especially as this was at the height of the normalization of the bourgeois idea of the domestic sphere, with the mother as the angel of the house and the father as the public-facing disciplinarian, professional, or worker. For example, at a similar time, many of the elite British modernists had queer polyamorous relationships. The controlling image of the patriarchal family was used to police other forms of relationship and sex, particularly with the lower classes, racialized and colonized people, and perceived same-sex relationships, but this surveillance usually did not come for the aristocracy. Of course, the image wasn't the reality. People acted in all kinds of ways outside the norms, some of them being punished with incarceration in prisons or psychiatric hospitals or even killed. (Oscar Wilde's punishment for gross indecency occurred almost at the same time that Prime Minister Archibald Primrose was having an affair with a man, but only one situation was prosecuted in court.) The anarchist perspective on relationships politicizes the desire that drives connections between people (or acknowledges that desire is politicized).

In his science fiction novel, *Trouble on Triton*, Samuel Delany has a character—a doctor helping someone transition genders—explain the current thought on best childcare practices: "Our current superstition—and it seems to work, out here—is that a child should have available at least five close adult attachments—that's living, loving, feeding, and diaper-changing attachments—preferably with five different sexes." Note the word "superstition," too, which admits that this approach is just a cultural product, not definite knowledge. Its practice relies only on its apparent effectiveness. Delany simply multiplies the number of caregivers and genders of the people who look after children. If we reconsider supporting the growth of a child, removing the concern of biological parentage lets us see that all children benefit from a number of loving connections in their life. We can extend this to our grown selves too, unlimiting our expectations of attachment and intensity, so that we can find different scenarios to nurture different aspects of ourselves.

Looking to science fiction, we find so many different visions of how to arrange better forms of childcare, work, and family life. In *Woman on the Edge of Time*, Marge Piercy depicts a society in which there are three "mothers" with no gender, all of whom breastfeed, none of whom carry the child, and there is a ceremony of separation for the child after which they take a break of contact from their mothers. Ursula K. Le Guin's *The Dispossessed* includes a picture that might be familiar to people who studied 1960s liberatory movements, with a communalized care system for children, where parents and children don't live or sleep together (in fact everyone typically sleeps alone unless they decide to "bunk" together for a night or so).

But these various approaches to living together aren't simply science fiction. They more accurately represent the realities of how we are brought up, especially the further we are from the normalized Christian whiteness of Western Europe. Most of us actually live outside the controlling image of the nuclear family. In the same way, we can interrogate the structures of care and kinship against the enforced labor of living under capitalism, rejecting the norms that end up isolating us in miserable families and shun the help of community care in order to rethink the possibilities of families, children, and adults and the lives we all lead.

Andie Nordgren uses the term "relationship anarchy" to rethink our approaches to relationships of all kinds, not exclusively romantic. A main point of this philosophy is to reject the notion that our love and care is a scarce resource (here there are echoes also with the forced scarcity of capitalism), which we can only devote to one or a few people. Similarly, Nordgren pushes us to rethink the hierarchy of relationships, which tends to use romantic partnership or marriage to eclipse friendships. If you look at all of your relationships from the same level, you can more intentionally interact with them and not feel like giving your time to one means demoting or promoting another, all while acknowledging that your time and energy and connections can fluctuate over time. You can have a partner and close friends without feeling like they vie for all of you. You can have your inner "pod" of friends, as well as people you interact with more infrequently or with different boundaries. You can integrate solitude, too.

Polyamory is commonly upheld as a truly anarchist form of romantic entanglement, which gets practiced in various ways, from primary partnership and even domestic co-living with room to explore other relationships, to a sort of "single" life filled with many different sexual or romantic relationships that are not exclusive of one another. Often, anarchists will imbue polyamory with an ethical imperative over the mainstream norm of (hetero)sexual monogamy, since it seems to sidestep the property relations that are realized in possession of another person (marriage), not to mention the idea of the passage of property through blood and family lines (procreation). However, polyamory contains its own traps and isn't inherently liberatory. We have to extend polyamory to mean that the act of loving itself ought not to be seen as hierarchical, that our love for a "partner" does not need to overshadow our love for someone who is "just a friend," or simply erase the possibility of other deep relationships. Neither does a commitment to biological family have to outweigh support for our "chosen" families.

Facing the Mess of Our Lives

Ultimately, an anarchist approach to relationships also tries to understand the messiness of life. Our lives don't fit the stories we have been told about them. The concept of sexuality that we are given is completely entangled in power dynamics. Even the swindle of romance narratives that prime us for unrealistic expectations of partnership shows this—

our culture depicts every aspect of romantic/sexual relationships except how people can actually take care of each other. We need to leave room for the unknown, the unknowable—we are mysteries even to ourselves. This messiness has been discussed at length by prison abolitionists and transformative justice/community accountability practitioners. It usually comes up in answer to a similar critique that anarchists face: so you want to get rid of prisons/the market/the state? Well, what will you replace it with? The bad faith is in the question, which, in line with state thinking of centralized, singular, eternal solutions, imagines that every problem has one answer that can be generalized and applied in every situation. The answer for abolitionists and anarchists is that there could be a multitude of loosely networked, autonomous community-based responses to problems instead of prisons, and social organization and collective care rather than the state. We improvise our solutions as events demand, and the things that work we might try again with slight modifications. But we don't need to turn every action into an eternal law—or even into the way our modern law works through a paradox of rules and interpretations, all made hierarchically. Similarly, we can look at our lives without trying to jam them into the contours of a neat narrative of development, professionalization, coupling, achievement, and success. When we judge ourselves against our perceptions of others, we lose the texture of daily life, all the parts that fall outside the contours, the edges. We forget that there is no right way to live, that we improvise life every day: attempts and failures, connection and conflict, joy and grief. Everything moves, and we move through it.

Utopian thinking often gets dismissed for scrubbing out the "real" problems that we face. If capitalist economics tell us that life is a war of all against all, and every man must fend for himself, utopians get ridiculed for imagining a human nature that is good, cooperative, empathetic—perfect, and ultimately then dead, because it does not involve conflicting desires. But that picture is not what anarchists or abolitionists are actually proposing when they think about a different world. Getting rid of the state, of prisons, of the market doesn't solve all of our problems. It just solves the imbalance of power that those institutions hold. People will still mess up, hurt each other, change their minds, learn, and grow. People will still want different things—people will still be different from each other, but perhaps those differences won't be systematized into a hierarchy of class, gender, or race. We need space to work from the bottom up rather than imposing top-down expectations, laws, and violence to control things that don't go as they are supposed to.

Starting with our initial relationships to those closest to us—setting our boundaries and observing boundaries set by others—allows our habits, practices, miscommunications, projected feelings, and other seeds of conflict to become clearer to our eyes, and then to be discussed between us. All of this takes work, to practice, as June Jordan calls it, "responsibility without power." But it's not the kind of work involved in our jobs, where we are exploited, chewed up, and spat out (more on that later). It's the work of love, of building connections, of understanding, which is messy and often painful but then often creates stronger bonds when you face conflict—or enables your self-determination when you break up. It might be easier said than done, especially since most of us are wounded, both in our immediate lives and in the intergenerational trauma we carry in our bodies. But to shift our perspective in how we relate to one another in the way that I'm suggesting allows more space to back up from how our loved ones act and react, so that we don't get caught up in our own reactions. We can then see how each one of us is trying our best both to get what we need and show up for others, and then we can release each other from the impossible demands of perfect behavior.

The perspective of abolitionists and the theory behind transformative justice shows that harm is systematized, and in many ways the harm we enact interpersonally is a reflection of our enmeshment in these systems of harm. The transformation that transformative justice demands is in the conditions that made the harm possible in the first place. Let's address our relationships within these larger contexts of harm, so that we no longer burden the single individual with the sole responsibility of causing and accounting for the harm done. But neither do we absolve people for causing harm. Instead, we use the conflicts that we face as opportunity to disidentify with the systems we have been born into and brought up through.

It is almost impossible for any of us to escape these systems unharmed and non-traumatized, whether it's from direct state violence or the pain and suffering of the nuclear family. In other words, we are all in various ways, to various degrees, messed up, used up, exhausted, and often impatient. When we have so little, we sometimes hold our pain and trauma close. It's familiar. We are harmed, and that familiar harm shows up in our interpersonal relationships. We harm each other in ways that we've been harmed. However, we also have a tendency to avoid conflict, to avoid working through the problems that come between us, to be afraid of communication that is difficult (see how this affects even, say, white people's willingness to have real discussions about racism and how they even unintentionally uphold the workings of white supremacy). People will more willingly call the police than ask their neighbors to turn their music down. Abolitionists call this approach "carceral logic," where we seek punishment for people who diverge from us in various way. We defer to an external authority rather than confront a problem ourselves. We punish each other because of the ways we are cut out of connection. Or we condemn out of our own fear of being condemned (what gets called cancel culture out of control). I can speak from experience in saying that in the midst of crisis, perhaps in my intimate relationships, I often feel too ashamed to reach out for community help. And perhaps many people would think they do not know how to respond. But my experience also has shown me that given the chance most people show up for each other with care when called upon in crisis—and can improvise unforeseen solutions.

If we can separate for a moment our relationships from the power systems they operate within, we can try to differentiate our embodiment of these power systems from our ability to disidentify from them. I want to insist through this book that the structure of power doesn't saturate every instant of our lives. If we collapse ourselves into the state-sanctioned forms of power—including perhaps most importantly the identities imposed upon us—we ultimately lose our freedom to remove ourselves from them.

Maintaining relationships also includes knowing that we will cause others pain, even unintentionally, and that honoring the relationship demands a way to address differing experience. Furthermore, this process of accounting for ourselves allows us to explore our relationships, to find out what we really want. We should be accountable to the relationship, to what we want to do with it, as well as to the larger community that it exists within—and we need to make these expectations explicit through our modes of communication. Ultimately, we can see what is worthwhile for us to put our time and energy into and that we can release ourselves from relationships just as easily as we can put more effort into growing and building them.

Community and Care

But before we get too starry eyed, we have to think a bit more about what we mean by "community," since many of us feel completely isolated due to the demands of work, family life, and the impulse for disconnection. In the dreams of community accountability, community would be people with shared space and affinity who can act as a container for harm, thereby allowing for a conflict to be resolved whereby the person who caused harm can grow and be accountable and the person who was harmed has support without alienation. The reality of harm often fractures whatever fragile community there is, especially when dynamics of gender and race come into play, such that the person who is harmed ends up isolated, afraid to go to places the person who harmed them might be, and feeling unsupported. Employment, prestige and popularity, and perceived power differentials can all affect who gets heard and who gets supported. The pod-mapping exercise described by Mia Mingus and the Bay Area Transformative Justice Collective is one way to counteract the nebulousness of community by giving us a way to organize our relationships according to the actual connections we have with others. We are asked to think of the different relationships we have and which people we will call on for what needs of support—including the worst crises. When we start drawing this out on a piece of paper, we see the networks we exist in, which may be multiple "communities" that intersect and overlap or ones that don't touch at all. We also begin to articulate the kinds of relationships we have with specific people: we might bring one person a problem we wouldn't mention to another.

For the person who causes harm, there is rarely the support or incentive for admitting making a mistake. Often, even the communities that talk about abolishing punitive culture and using transformative methods to resolve conflicts will still think in terms of punishment, ostracization, or simply calling people out for causing harm. And many people are reluctant to try to remove a person who has harmed from the spaces and positions where they can exercise power. I want to be clear, I believe there are certainly instances where calling out harm is necessary, especially to protect other people from being harmed. Similarly, I believe that ostracization can be a powerful tool. And in my own experience, I have dealt with people who seem so committed to harm and preying on vulnerable people that I don't think there are any real ways to help them transform (barring a radical change in their own perspective). But I've also had the experience that the services the state offers to people who are harmed, especially ones who are more vulnerable due to racism, (trans)misogyny, or sexual discrimination, do not actually aim to protect or support those people. The whole process of pursuing legal action often leaves the person who has been harmed more vulnerable and rarely ends in a long-term strategy for survival. In the end, whether the authorities are called in or an accountability process is started, the person who caused harm often can just move on without any form of accountability, or even turn the processes and institutions to their own advantage.

While there are plenty of takedowns of cancel culture, especially recently, it has been a tool used by groups most vulnerable to state violence, like Black queer/trans people, to keep themselves safe. There is a power in naming harm, since so much of it is normalized. Certain levels of abuse or harm are just part and parcel of being a child, a spouse, a lover, a student, or an employee. Anarchist approaches to relationships fit into these traditions of naming harm, from Black feminist, queer/trans, and Indigenous practices—all approaches that work outside or beyond of the state's purview. And I would add this doesn't preclude an understanding that some people will not transform, be held account-able, or stop harming, and that there is a need for collective self-defense against these people, whatever that looks like, from ostracization, deplatforming, or revenge.

But again, this is a messy business. One might object that maintaining relationships and building community in this way involves a huge amount of work. We are often so tired out and absorbed by the basic labor of making money to pay for subsistence, there's not much time left for anything else. However, this division of the labor of the wage from what Marxist feminists name "reproductive" labor (the work necessary to maintain life, which is most often unpaid and thoroughly feminized) is also a tactic of racial capitalism, just as the division of gender and the creation of a hierarchy of races is. The long process of removing people from lifeways that allowed for them to survive as communities is the history of the violent imposition of capitalism and the state. There are countless stories of how this was done, from the enclosure of common land, to the gendering of different kinds of work, to the creation of dependence on wage labor to purchase the things necessary for life, to the creation of centralized food systems and monoculture that eliminated people's ability to grow their own food. We must simulta-neously acknowledge that maintaining life is real "work" and support ourselves and others in this necessary task while also aiming to abolish the relation of work under capitalism, which is necessarily a relationship of exploitation. How often do you wish you could just live rather than work, even if just living isn't easy?

We might shift the emphasis, then, from one of the "work" of maintaining relationships and building that seemingly mythical com-munity to one of care. Or we can put them together to note that the care work we do can be rethought both as a form of labor and a revolu-tionary drive to reframe the important parts of our lives. In *Care Work: Dreaming Disability Justice*, disability justice organizer, Leah Lakshmi Piepzna-Samarasinha looks into ways to "build emergent, resilient care webs," with a focus on the way that people who are chronically ill, or dealing with mental illness or different kinds of disabilities, have had to generate their own networks of care in their community. Especially for

Black and Indigenous people, and people of color—different identities that have been differently racialized and criminalized by the state—the limited state services available don't always provide effective aid to make life livable, whether it's in terms of transportation, support for food and living costs, or other minimal supports for those who can't fit into the capitalist frames of labor and productivity. The discussion of disability gets shunted to the side or internalized with guilt and shame so often. I am a chronically ill person, and have had to surreptitiously build my entire life around the needs and possibilities of flares of my illness, which impede me from holding down regular work. I've been lucky with the access I've had, but it also takes infinite amounts of time in a for-profit healthcare system to navigate things to your own benefit. Many people get lost in the shuffle, not to mention the fact that chronic illness and disabilities often overlap with other forms of exclusion. I have a community willing to care for me, but even reaching out for basic help comes with such a feeling of failure.

Piepzna-Samarasinha foregrounds "the revolution work we do when we cook a meal for each other." People thrust into the movement work of organizing and activism will often overlook the needs of care, whether it's food, childcare, or even necessities of health and comfort. Piepzna-Samarasinha asks, then, "what does it mean to shift our ideas of access and care (whether it's disability, childcare, economic access, or many more) from an individual chore, an unfortunate cost of having an unfortunate body, to a collective responsibility that's maybe even deeply joyful?" We can't ignore disability, as many revolutionaries do (in a eugenicist or genocidal way), especially because, as Piepzna-Samarasinha writes, "all of us will become disabled and sick, because state systems are failing." Instead, we can shift away from the term work to rediscover the deep joy she mentions in the seemingly simple tasks of helping each other meet our basic needs while actually receiving support and care.

As for the work part of caring, Piepzna-Samarasinha imagines a "fair trade exchange" of feminized emotional labor. This exchange highlights the need to recognize limits of what you can take on for another person. But the simple revolutionary response Piepzna-Samarasinha notes for the kind of care work we do for each other can even just be recognition and gratitude (if not actual monetary wages for housework). We are so used to placing the emphasis on productivity for the job market and capitalist economy that we shift our view away from the actual fact of living and what we need to do that. Ostensibly, we work to afford those basic necessities, but then life just slips by. Of course, it's no coincidence that the work of living is feminized, racialized, and invisibilized. But in this vein, I push us to imagine our liberation in entering this space and taking on this work—the actual web of social relations—as the very act of living.

FAQs

Do I have to be polyamorous?

Short answer: you don't have to do anything you don't want to. But some anarchists (and other people) try to act like polyamory is the only revolutionary way to envisage romantic entanglement, undoing the property relations that undergird heterosexual relationships like marriage. However, a good anarchist wouldn't prescribe a single practice for everyone. You can still enjoy being in a couple or monogamy while working to undo the way we have been taught that love means choosing a single person to meet all of your needs forever and losing the importance of other relationships. Of course, you can also find ways to do many different, multiple relationships that honor and respect the needs of each person involved, or not define yourself at all through romantic or sexual relationships.

What if I am missing out?

Anarchism can help solve FOMO (the fear of missing out). This fear takes over when you are at the moment of upholding a boundary. When you want to leave a social situation, or say no to an invitation, your mind evokes all the possible fun you might have. This fear leads you to engage in activities you don't want, and to lose moments of solitude and rest that could replenish you. Social media has amplified our FOMO, because we are privy to curated images of lifestyles we imagine are superior to the mundanity of actual living. In bringing intentionality into our relationships by understanding our boundaries, we can use these platforms to find ways of foregrounding care and kindness and refuse to model the behaviors they promote.

3

You Call This Living?
Anarchy on the Job

- You aren't your job
- Give up on competition and climbing the ladder
- Steal back your time and their resources

The Myth of Work

In Chapter 2, we touched on the gendered aspects of work that get invisibilized in family and care. In *Full Surrogacy Now*, Sophie Lewis points to the so-called "natural" parts of life—everything we do to survive, to care for each other, to continue making humans—and insists we must name all of this as work, but "from the point of view of the struggle against work." That is, from the perspective of abolishing work as a defining social relation. Perhaps the ultimate denaturalization we must aim for is the myth that surrounds work, since it is inextricably bound to the other forms of hierarchy and control that order our world: gender, race, and class. Moreover, the emphasis on work even from a left perspective has always obscured the networks of care and mutual support that have actually sustained our lives. In the end, we don't want to work, we want to live.

There have been many critiques of the leftist tendency to fantasize about the worker and their revolutionary potential, especially coming from feminist, queer, and Black radical perspectives. A certain "class reductionism" frames the priority of revolutionary movement as the struggle of economic class through the struggle at work and considers "identity" markers as secondary aspects of revolution. But more to the point, the image of the worker tends to uphold a masculine image that dovetails nicely with conservative, even patriotic images of the working class that ignores the way work is part of the enforcement of racial and gender hierarchies, not to mention just a dominant and awful part of our lives. This image of the white worker is the same repertoire that army and police recruitment comes from. A mistake of working-class pride is to worship the chains that oppress us. Anarchists want a world without work.

A common argument made by both the left and the right is that without some kind of regime of enforcement for labor, everyone would just be lazy and nothing would get done. It's true that forcing people to work can get things done, but it doesn't account for the way people work at activities that matter to them and the people they love. The same perspective about the need for coercion argues that unhoused people must be on the streets because of their own laziness, or perhaps their use of alcohol or other substances. We classify people based on how they appear, and as Oyěwùmí remarks, we believe this hierarchical society provides an "accurate reflection" of where people belong. We are trained to have an innate reverence for "work," and yet there is also a clear denigration of "workers" that is part and parcel of the same culture. The whole mythology of pulling yourself up was premised on a system of slave labor, capturing people from Africa and forcing them into the situation of property and racialized subordination, along with the theft of lands and genocide of Indigenous inhabitants. The reality of work actually tends towards the ideal of a generalized enforced labor. We do more and more for less and less and barely scrape by.

Slavery is a necessary adjunct of capitalism. Not only is it a fact that all the accumulated wealth of the so-called industrialized (or post-industrialized) countries has been plundered from colonized and subjugated lands—as Fanon writes, "Europe is literally the creation of the third world. The riches which are choking it are those plundered from the underdeveloped peoples"—but in lands like the USA, the literal infrastructure was built by an enslaved population that was forced to work and unable to claim the fruits of their labor. This dispossession—double in terms of theft of land/resources and theft of life/freedom—laid the groundwork for any semblance of a working economy that we still discuss in pseudo-scientific terms today. Capitalism needs slavery in order to remain profitable for the owners. Even after the abolition of legalized slavery, its afterlife has consisted of a racialized division of labor, despite liberal diversity whitewashing, that maintains a perpetual underclass.

The ideology of capitalism is that the laborer is free to sell their labor on the market in exchange for a fair wage that will enable them to buy the things they need to survive. This ideology masks the actual fact of this arrangement: that it's a system consisting of warfare. The managers of the economy see the population—the workers—as a problem, always wanting more and threatening the lives of the rich. The fact of a codependence that actually allows for survival and thriving gets shifted into a story of minority and majority, of dependency and paternalism.

A central tenet of the ideology of capitalism as an organization of society and economy builds on an idea of incentivization through money and goods, alongside "healthy" competition, that creates the most productivity. This argument assumes there is a simple human nature that is lazy, and so workers have to be basically tricked into working. You can go back into history to understand this from another angle, since the historical process of capitalist dominance involved forcing people to work for wages by violently removing them from the other life ways they were embedded in (not that these were all necessarily romantic and liberated). In other words, a situation had to be created that forced people to work and trick them that it was in their self-interest (survival) rather than the boss's (profit). Even in the so-called communist countries (i.e. state communism or state capitalism), work wasn't the promised liberated space—they replicated state hierarchies, with workers continuing forms of drudgery in the push for "modernization." Anarchists might bring us to question the idea of technological development, industrialization, and modernization as a goal that should be universalized without question, or rather that any of these things are unidirectional, evenly applied forces.

The people who defend capitalism as the only natural way to get people to work will also argue that this drive is the source of all of our comforts and technological innovations. They use this argument to make claims for future innovations that will supposedly make life better, but that will actually be turned into commodities and turned over to corporate profits. And they generalize this idea to past technologies, claiming they could only have come about through capitalist-driven innovation. This perspective disguises the reality of innovation under an unfalsifiable claim. While they can't prove that whatever technology we have is simply due to capitalist economic forces, we also can't say, "well, in an alternative history, where all societies are organized outside of states and hierarchies, etc. (anarchism or communism), there would still be technological achievements." It's true that industrialization and technological development have brought comforts to many people's lives—but again, the benefits are unevenly distributed, and are entangled with further immiseration, coercive labor, and environmental destruction.

The technological underpinnings of Western societies—the very ideology of technology—is inextricable from the forms of domination that nation states have imposed. But still, the underlying reality of most innovations can most often be traced to some version of collective work or resource sharing, even if that means being directly propped up by the state in terms of funding. The ideal of scientific discovery is anarchistic—a decentralized society of people experimenting and testing things out to see what works and what doesn't. Yet, the narratives about discovery (and history) tend to identify single people—the great men—as responsible for every leap forward, obscuring the fact that none of these things happen in a vacuum, and this individualist history just plays into the incentivizing of our commitment to the endless wheel of work. Moreover, profit-driven innovation leads to developing commodities that make more money, not necessarily things that make life better for (most) people. On top of that, much of the capital behind innovation gets shuttled through the military, so that technological development is actually tied into perfecting the means of destroying life, not improving it.

The technological dream of automation causes much confusion for liberatory visions. The idea of full automation is that technology will eventually free us from the most menial forms of labor, by replacing human working hours with machine work. If machines do the cleaning, for example, I have more free time to enjoy myself. But the capitalist reality of automation is that machines replace workers, who don't get paid time off, just unemployment. Utopian visions, like Oscar Wilde's anarchist-inflected "The Soul of Man under Socialism," imagine an automated future where all necessities are machine-driven, leaving most people to work a minimal amount of hours and devote the rest of their lives to self-expression. This kind of vision gets parodied in the term "fully automated luxury communism." A certain vision of socialism, centralized and state-based, sees technological development leading towards (the possibility) of liberation from work. However, this idea isn't far from the liberal thinking at the turn of the twentieth century that believed scarcity could be ended—a belief belied by entrenched ideas of racial hierarchies. One can't help but notice that the vision of full automation is a subtly transmuted version of slavery. Wilde acknowledges this in his fully automated vision: the machines doing the work merely replicate the systems of slavery that have always undergirded so many ideas of freedom. Arguably, the capitalist idea of work has so infected our relationship to what goes into living in this world that we can't imagine freedom without forcing someone or something to work for us. Inherent to this vision is a degrading of certain forms of work—menial labor, cleaning, domestic labor—while uplifting more important work.

Work Has No Moral Value

A truism that seems to afflict the current workers (read: consumers) of the world is that "there is no ethical consumption under capitalism." We have grown up in a world full of problems created by the collaboration of states and corporations that then get individualized as consumer-based solutions—as if we could buy our way out of the corruption, or not buying something would somehow counteract the devastating effect on the planet and lives that these states and corporations wield. So we are left with the understanding that there is no way to completely avoid complicity in the disastrous aspects of capitalism, as for the most part we are given no choice of survival by other means. This feeling can lead us to a despair at the possibility of any transformation. Even if we can individually escape (some of) the complicity in various ways, that doesn't affect the other people kept under the thumb of working to survive. So let's push this slogan further: the counterpart to "no ethical consumption under capitalism" is that there is "no ethical work under capitalism."

At this point, most young people have experienced first hand that the chance of "making it" in any recognizable way is nearly impossible. I write as a person on the millennial cusp with a middle-class background. I pursued academia, given that it provided me with income temporarily and seemed like better work than office jobs. I bought into the myth of the "vocation": that I was called to this work and that it was inherently valuable, that I'd be joining a community of scholars who are driven by the desire to produce knowledge and transform the world for the better. The 2008 crash occurred while I was in grad school, which, if I needed any other wakeup call to my rosy picture of a profession marked by genuine interest in intellectual collaboration, proved that getting any kind of secure job in the field I had dedicated my life to was next to impossible. Of course, if I had opened my eyes a bit more, I would have seen that hardly anyone was involved out of a genuine interest in learning or sharing radical world-changing ideas—it was a world of competition for scarce resources and an ever elusive job security in tenure. The university is run like a business and the faculty live in an imaginary castle of importance while they continually cede power to profit-seeking administration. I'm not even touching on the implications of the university in the legacies of slavery and Indigenous genocide. Quickly, I took up my place in the so-called "precariat": the former "professions" that have become ever more casualized. When I do teach college students, I acknowledge that they are taking on massive debt to achieve access to a world of jobs that just doesn't exist.

Almost everyone I know works in service, mostly in restaurants and bars. Those who don't have to hustle in some way to make enough to pay rent. At fancy colleges and business summits they call this hustle "entrepreneurship." It is the flashy side of the "gig economy," where people take on contractual work with no consistency under the guise of "freedom" from the 9–5 job. We need to be wary of the language that repackages precarity—the inability to find dependable work (and also access to services for subsistence)—as a kind of freedom, like being your own boss. In fact, many of the recent innovations in tech start-ups have further destroyed people's ability to form solidarity in the workplace. They quite often sell themselves through some aspect of anarchism and then refit it for a capitalist purpose. For example, the decentralization of Uber, or co-working spaces packaged as building community. (This kind of co-optation is also echoed in the way social media companies tout their community building while we passively generate profit for them.)

It's quite difficult to navigate our relationship to work since from all sides we get a moralizing/politicized discourse about our relationship to labor. The capitalist ideology that gets buoyed by a state that takes little to no responsibility for its citizens (despite what remnants of welfare or services remain) tells us this: work is a personal responsibility, it is a chance for us to make ourselves, to climb the social (class) ladder. Failure at work, or the inability to make a living, is a personal fault, not a systemic issue. Democracy means a level playing field where ascent comes through meritocracy; healthy competition is the strategy. On perhaps another level, work is framed for us throughout our education as a definitional aspect of our identity: what do you want to be when you grow up? Work goes alongside sexuality, gender, and race in building our capitalist/consumer identity. And in fact, our relationship to work is always a relationship to sex, gender, and race (and so is the history of how the idea of work has been imposed and enforced on massive populations). The jobs available to you are largely determined by your position in relation to the power structures that operate through race, gender, sexuality, and class.

Work and Revolution

The anarchist understanding of work is that it is an enforced situation, a relationship of oppression. Work will not make us free. For us, it is another area of disidentification; we should give up the idea of labor as a proof of self-worth and discard fantasies of making it, of finding ourselves, of loving work so much that there is no distinction between our operating hours and our off time. Instead we need to relate to the necessity of work in order to survive in our current conditions from a different perspective that takes the value away from work itself, whether it is perceived as being noble due to its manual labor or its seeming alignment with your ethical values.

Anarchism exists in the interstices, unseen by official time, and helps us replace the emphasis in our lives on the off-moments where the sense of freedom that can really drive our movements exists in our real daily experience. We are plugged into wage labor through the idea that work time is compensated with an abstract, ever-plunging monetary value, whatever minor income we are able to wrest from employers. The Benjamin Franklin adage, "time is money," comes to claim our time, the time of the clock—punching in to work, accountable hours, keycards to leave for the bathroom, eating while working, receiving messages all day long with demanded response times. The division of the day into 24 hours, with 60 minutes, 60 seconds, infinitesimally divides our time into an empty container we are expected to fill with productivity, though often our work consists of waiting out the clock. But none of these accountings of time actually contain the moments of our lives: the downtime, the time of care and reprieve, and the moments lived in resistance to being seen, being known, being at work, being surveilled.

We might claim these moments of "life" are those lived in anarchy, which aren't accounted for. Time to feel grounded in your body without movement or purpose. Time for the endless involuntary process of breathing, the mixture of interior and exterior, where the world fills us and leaves us every moment. A time of nourishment in eating, time sitting outside looking. Not the dead time of commuting, though it's possible to catch a glimpse when you are pulled out of the ordering of your own life: perhaps a chance encounter on the bus, or at least the ability to see all the kinds of people that exist in their strangeness.

The contradictions of work became extremely clear as soon as the pandemic hit. Workers were divided into "essential workers," who were expected to risk their lives—and this category included healthcare workers as well as service workers, containing its own contradiction of classes—and people who could work from home, with the final categories being people who were fired or furloughed. Many countries issued pandemic payments to people, demonstrating the possibility of just giving workers money to supplement the meager incomes that actual jobs pay.

As many people were forced to stay at home and not to work, one of the things the situation of the pandemic drove home is how many of the jobs we do could simply disappear without affecting the world (at least not negatively). People were forced to figure out living in different ways—at home, without work, without access to the same things, including necessary care networks, sometimes in dangerous situations, sometimes in relative comfort, still contained by the encasement of technology, Netflix, Instagram, etc. Despite the real fear (and fearmongering) that accompanied the pandemic, I had initially hoped that the sudden radical change of how everything worked would have a larger impact on people's willingness to put up with the layered systems that keep us working harder and harder for less and less. I started working with people to organize a rent strike, since it seemed like such a blatant contradiction that we were still expected to pay our rent with no income. But this attempt failed for a few reasons. As with labor organizing, there were no recent precedents of successful strikes. Similarly, there were no persistent structures or preceding actions within the neighboring community that made people feel they would actually be supported in sticking their necks out. Above all, the intense precariousness of life that most of us experience, which makes us grasp at anything that feels stable, stood in the way of people risking their homes.

On the other hand, what eventually did happen was a different sort of uprising, not in response to a pandemic enabled by global capitalism and nationalistic warmongering, but in anger after the police murder of George Floyd. Years of ever-heightening threats of white supremacy, anti-Blackness, racism, and anti-migrant sentiment stoked the flames that led to these uprisings, even if a single murder (one of many) was the final impetus. But we can still relate this uprising to the context of work. Our labor conditions may not be the tipping point to ending the complex systems of oppression, though arguably being out of work—and being involved in mutual aid—does seem to connect to the willingness to risk more when the racist violence becomes intolerable. For many, the pandemic precarity wasn't new, just a solidified version of a long-term experience: tinder that needed a spark. On a hopeful note, the authors of the essay, "The Interregnum: The George Floyd Uprising, the Coronavirus Pandemic, and the Emerging Social Revolution," argue that the phenomena after the uprising of the "Great Resignation," which they rename the "Great Refusal," of people giving up their low-paid, pointless jobs, was a furthering of the revolutionary fervor of the rebellion into more aspects of our daily life. They argue that moving from a questioning of police and prisons to a refusal to work generalizes the rebellion to the everyday, helping move the "political revolution," which still risks being contained by the state and authoritarian leftist parties, towards a "social revolution," which threatens to destroy the hierarchies of society as we know it. The important note here is that the Great Resignation or Refusal has happened, worldwide, outside of the normal channels of labor organizing, in a spontaneous yet still concerted way.

Repurpose Your Work Life

We are taught from a young age to find work that will make us happy, but work can't make us happy in this system. Thus, we should give up that impossible dream. Sure, a lucky few can have jobs that give them relative freedom or that contribute a small amount to a larger struggle. Relieving ourselves of the pressure of finding ourselves through our work frees us up to relate to our jobs differently.

Most likely we don't work under conditions that would allow us to overthrow our bosses. But we can still understand that we don't owe our bosses anything. The anonymous anarchist collective Crimethinc declared April 15 to be "Steal Something from Work Day"—a good anarchist holiday, since we need our own rituals. As bosses profit off our labor in excess of what they actually pay us, Crimethinc suggests taking what we need: "You earned it!" They see this as a potentially collective process too: "Work together to maximize your under-the-table profit-sharing; make sure all of you are safe and getting what you need." They note that we already most likely do steal from work, if only in non-productive work time (scrolling on our phones, longer-than-necessary bathroom breaks). Even simply taking a paperclip can help us see that we are permitted to do this.

Instead of traditional labor organizing as the main point of resistance, we can create alternative networks of relationship, care, and theft through work, covering for each other in all the ways we can. Certain workplaces foster a spirit of competition; our responsibility to each other would be to counteract this mindset. It's easy to get annoyed when someone else doesn't seem to "pull their weight," but that perspective relies on the assumption that everyone has equal means, or starts from the same position of ability, access, and comfort. We need to start from the understanding that no one wants to be at work, that we are all eking out an existence within an enforced system of labor that actually takes us away from the things we'd prefer to do, and mostly we are doing work that isn't strictly necessary for the continuation of life. Then we can look at someone's so-called laziness as a more reasonable response than the unchecked dedication that star employees model.

In Chapter 2, we looked at the home as a space where we can proactively practice care and conflict resolution—these same relational models can be used to disrupt the power systems at work. We can approach people we work with from a caring perspective while keeping in mind that we are forced to be there and the management structure and the boss are not allies. In other words, the care that you put into the "reproduction of life," that is, just being able to live, is different than the care you put into a workplace that doesn't treat you well—but even in our places of work, we are still trying to live. So we can't just discount work as a meaningless part of our day but as another source of life where we could live otherwise. Thus, we refuse to perform surveillance on behalf of the bosses and counteract the ways we are separated and individualized at work by finding ways to collaborate to ease everyone's burden.

At work, we practice another form of disidentification, removing our investment in the structures of reward that keep us putting all of our life and energy into work—when really all we need from work is the money to survive. Can we shift the meaning we are supposed to derive from work as part of our identity towards the meaning we can derive from taking what (scraps) work gives us that we can repurpose towards our communities? Can we create solidarity with the other workers in this situation, not to have better work but to have better lives in general? For example, when I had access to institutional funds at a college, I tried to use the money to pay people in the community doing liberatory work. But also, I tried to leverage whatever prestige my position gave me to promote anyone else who could use it. If you get your foot in the door, kick it open and let as many people in as you can. (For me, this could be by writing recommendation letters, serving as a reference with my accreditation, signing off on things that excuse people from unnecessary expectations so they can get on living their lives, giving everyone A's, and so on).

Our job lives are processes of indoctrination where we are asked to see ourselves as part of a team, contributing to a common mission. However, we know this is not the case, as we can be fired at will by a single person, and our performance is evaluated against the work of others, fostering competition not cooperation. Most workplaces are structured in the same hierarchies that we see in our governments, our heteronormative families, our racist society, and so the supposed team is always split against itself. Not only are we kept in line by the fear of destitution, we also constantly have a carrot in front of our faces of better prospects if only ... we work harder.

There have been countless arguments against the idea that people will only work if forced to do so, or incentivized by the wage, not to mention the basic need for survival. The current state of our lives makes it hard to imagine living otherwise, and therefore makes it easier for us to believe the lie of laziness, if only because we seem to be faced with the options of work or starve. And we do feel lazy, but that's because we spend so much of our time doing tiring, underpaid, undervalued, meaningless labor. From that perspective, everything seems exhausting. And if we think of work in that way, no one would want to do it. But we do find wellsprings of passion when we do things that feel meaningful, even if the world at large doesn't recognize it that way. Now those moments of feeling meaningful remain fleeting and sparse, in comparison to the drudgery of working, living without support and care, striving to get by. Yet they always do exist even in the midst of misery, and these are also cracks that point to the other world we aim for as anarchists.

There are other anarchist endeavors to rethink work, such as forming collectively owned worker cooperatives, where a particular business is owned by all the people involved, making decisions based on consensus, sharing income equally, and so on. There has also been a resurgence in more traditional anarchist labor organizing, in the guise of a revamped Industrial Workers of the World, organizing in all kinds of labor sectors including fast food restaurants and inside prisons. Some of us may even still be involved in "productive" labor, like industrial production or warehousing and distribution (like the burgeoning sector of Amazon workers), making or supplying some of the commodities that people need within this system to live. We can see organizing along the classic union lines as a means of survival within these situations. There has been a spate of successful labor strikes along the old models, in healthcare by nurses, in schools by teachers, and more. We ought not to dismiss any of these campaigns, and it is important for anarchists to lend solidarity to projects of workers determining their conditions for themselves. However, we also need to recognize that many of these efforts end up reproducing the conditions of work itself and therefore limit the horizon of life.

Ultimately, the anarchist argument has to be for the abolition of work. In this word, we understand the hierarchical relationship of worker to boss, which is one of exploitation, devoting the surplus value (profit) to the boss at the expense of the worker. Whatever we do in some anti-capitalist version of society, then, wouldn't be (called) work. As proposed in Chapter 2, I argue that we rethink our social relations in terms of care, since care is what enables us to live and forges the connections with other people in interdependency. Work retains too much of the religious moralism of proving one's goodness, if not all the other trappings of competition and individualism of capitalism. What we do in the world could instead be framed as a kind of love: for ourselves, for others, for the world itself.

But beyond work, we also have to change our understanding of luxury and leisure. In our current system, leisure, our time off, is actually part of the structure of work. The transition from a culture of production to one of consumption works through the understanding that we work in order to buy. Thinkers like Adorno and Horkheimer have argued that this structure extends to culture itself, where the entertainment that we take in on our off time is just a perpetuation of our relationship of exploitation to work. The sitcom is a perfect example. In our downtime we watch TV stories about people working, living in families, trying to have relationships, and laugh at all absurdity of it, while we are also caught up in the same structures, causing an endless circle of representation, prescription, and entrapment. There is little difference between the TV sitcom nuclear family or work family. Everywhere we look, the normalization of this way of life assaults our senses, so that we see ourselves in these narratives against the evidence of our experience of hating work. Even for those of us who somewhat like what we do for money can acknowledge that, without the need to earn to afford shelter and food, we probably wouldn't do these activities, at least not in this way.

Anarchist Luxury

What does luxury or leisure look like that isn't defined through work and access to goods we can purchase? (The other incentive of work is to buy all the best things.) Kristin Ross takes up the term "communal luxury" from the workers in the Paris Commune of 1871 (the Communards) as the title of her book evaluating that moment of another world: the Commune was situated outside and against the state and capitalism, in the midst of the height of industrialization, colonialism, and consolidation of the nation state. For these workers, poets, and thinkers, luxury meant the end to the division of labor, the separation of art from life, the distinction between thinking and working with your hands. This instance inspired anarchists like Kropotkin and Aesthetes like Oscar Wilde to describe a non-capitalist society where everyone is an artist—it wasn't an aspirational identity, or something only accessible to people who already have means. This shift also means that everyone could be seen as a worker, but the relationship of work under capitalism (alienation in Marxist terms) wouldn't persist. In fact, work would be seen as a totally different kind of social relation, the forging of relationships through making, sharing, and using. There, luxury blooms in a different way than we experience it now, in guilty pleasures, overspending, mass-produced culture like TV and movies—always consuming the work of alienated others.

Can we steal our time from work to dream of wanton liberation? It would take a huge leap to prepare everyone in small community units to reproduce life as it is. This means we would have to give up certain things for others. Removing our self-worth or self-definition—our very sense of self—from the relationship of work helps remove us from the domination of the relationship of work. It allows us to look at the remainder of our lives with fresh eyes and rethink how we might relate to the things we want, the things we love, the things that give us pleasure differently. It might ask us to go outside and see the world we are actually in, because not working changes our sense of time (dollars per hours) and space (home vs. job). While we are at work, not working, we could rethink ways to come together to fulfill those needs. We aren't waiting on a worker's revolution to overthrow the relation to work as enforcement. At least, in the meantime, let's steal from our bosses, steal our time away from work, steal ourselves from this system of domination, as much as possible, in order to rethink what living might be. Everything for everyone.

FAQs

Is it better to have a job I don't care about or a job I do care about?

You could argue either side of this! A job you don't care about might be easier to avoid identifying with in order to find meaning in your life. You might be able to keep the concerns of work separate from the life you actually want to live. On the other hand, while we are forced to work to survive, and work takes up so much time in our life, it makes sense to try to find ways to make that time less miserable. But if you do something you like for money, you need to guard more strenuously against identifying with work, especially if it is a job that carries some kind of cachet in society. If you do gain status, use it to help others access resources, and use any platform you have to speak out against power (and work itself!).

Would anything get done if we weren't made to work?

Capitalism makes us believe that people only work if incentivized through profit. But actually people like doing meaningful tasks that clearly connect to their lives and well-being. I use the term work to describe the system of exploitation under capitalism that forces us to do tasks that are disconnected from actual survival in order to earn money to pay for food, shelter, and care. Abolishing work doesn't mean everyone would be lazy do-nothings. It means we could engage in the things we want and need to do without being coerced. Sharing the labor of care and subsistence would allow more time to pursue creative activities, hobbies, and rest.

4

Can I Relearn That? Anarchy in School

We study with any person who can teach us.

Marge Piercy, *Woman on the Edge of Time*

- 'School teaches hierarchy, enforces individualism, and instills competition
- Study can take place anywhere
- The way we study helps make the world we want

Education in Hierarchy

Where it was established, free public education was seen ideologically as a gain of the end of the nineteenth century and beginning of the twentieth century, with the myth being that equal access to education would promote the possibility of upward mobility, as well as train students to be good citizens. However, when we combine this institutional ideology with the fact that, for a period of our lives, education is compulsory, we see that education is less about promoting freedom and status and rather about training citizens and workers of the state, and helping to instill the racial and gender hierarchies that structure the capitalist imperialist world. Though the introduction of free general public education came alongside labor struggles to shorten the workday and restrict child labor, as the state form consolidated itself amid these struggles, the school came to be a solution for the temporary warehousing of a population of youth who were not working and didn't have care,

73

and therefore operated rather as another kind of factory to produce citizens loyal to the country and ready to work.

Today, when the pathway to employment is nearly nonexistent and schools have been the site of endless culture wars of attrition, in which reactionary forces use a fear of liberal indoctrination to gut funding for state-run schools, the role of schools in our society becomes much starker. In other words, the school as a temporary warehousing of the young, to keep them off the streets and out of trouble, is more and more obvious. The education delivered by state-run schools has been optimized and streamlined through technocratic solutions so that it remains ultimately perfunctory. For racialized students, schools often have given up even that alibi of education, playing another role, described as "the school to prison pipeline," where Black and Brown students, as well as disabled students, get tracked from the earliest years of schooling through disciplining and profile, a long process of criminalization that exposes the intimate connection between schools and prisons.

Still, anarchists have long known that the ways we study have often been a vital tool of liberation, especially in informal, non-hierarchical situations embedded in life and movements. The important distinction to draw is that state-sponsored education as an institutional process, and knowledge as it is produced to uphold this context, do the work of maintaining our enthrallment to the way our lives are ordered. The difference of course is the institution and its relation to the state. In *Beyond Education*, Eli Meyerhoff tries to loosen the capture of study through schools and universities by thinking of learning in a larger context of "world-making and study," which happens by other means than the centralized ideas of programmatic, grade-based education. In his overview of the education system's history, he notes the ways education has continuously been used to defang popular resistance movements. This strategy parallels other concessions of access and inclusion, extending rights of participation in governing to an elite of a marginalized group, or in the case of education, to provide what has gotten framed as an unquestionable moral good and even a human right to everyone, but through a means of training them into the system that will exploit them.

An anarchist approach to study will ground our learning in community and collaboration against the individualized narrative of progress. There is a long history of anarchist alternative schools as well as theories of liberatory pedagogy, from early predecessors like William Godwin, to Francisco Ferrer's Modern School movement in Spain and then in the United States, to their legacy in free schools and other forms of collective processes and self-directed learning. In this chapter, I do not spend time telling the history of anarchist pedagogy and experiments in schooling. Instead, in the spirit of daily life, where we work within the contexts that we are given, I want to reframe ideas of study to imagine how a disidentification and counterknowledge can be produced in conjunction with each other in any time or place. In the world we currently live in, an anarchist approach to the education industrial complex would primarily be an approach of disidentifying from the structures the school naturalizes as the only form of life. Just as the family works as a laboratory of hierarchy, school works to imprint authority in a child's life. In fact, alongside the family, school plays a fundamental role in breaking the child from the richness of their emotional and imaginative life in order to make them fit into the norms of a hierarchical society. Much of education, then, whether informal or institutional, can be seen as a way to domesticate the child, replacing liberated possibilities with sanctioned values.

The teacher is the authority in the classroom. No matter how progressive an approach a teacher takes towards their students, the situation itself creates this power dynamic. The teacher can evacuate the power, but it still exists—I've discovered that in all the ways I've tried to contradict the hierarchy in my classroom but still have to grade students, for example. Or the ways that students fear communicating about their needs or problems, always fearing punishment for not being able to fit into the timelines and structures of curricula. We can extrapolate these forms of authority, from the family and school, to the bosses, to politicians, to police, to judges, and so on. Schools also internalize the bureaucratic logic that both governments and corporations use, where there is a seemingly decentralized network of responsible people (teachers, counselors) under the ultimate authority of a principal, a board of education, and so on. Teachers seem to have total power in the classroom, but they end up having to submit forms of assessment to these centralized boards. In "primary" education, this process leads to "teaching to the test" rather than a more tailored approach to engaging people in the process of studying together. Finally, politicians wield access to and the content of education as a political tool, with a constant threat to the livelihoods of teachers who don't obey. Teachers in state-run schools get burned out quickly unless they adapt themselves to the structures, relish wielding power over children, or find ways to engage children against the institutional demands.

Against the Individual Progress Narrative

The state education system works to consolidate a single narrative of life, history, and meaning. Ultimately, compulsory education works as a way to keep bodies in rooms under surveillance, instead of roaming the streets and getting into trouble. Of course, discipline is the main lesson of school: disciplining your body into order, not just in terms of breaking your body into forms of unnatural attention and posture but also as an amplification of the family work of instilling our gender, racialized, and sexual norms (did anyone else get picked on in school for their perceived gender and sexual deviance?). Our attention is demanded, our lives are regulated, and we are taught to regurgitate official knowledge that leaves out the fact that the state is always at war with us.

The mark of coercive education persists into university, even though many students choose college and a life of indebtedness in exchange for the hope of advancement. Transitioning from high school to college, even though this entails a huge payment of tuition (incursion of debt) and all the other costs of living that might seem to change one's relationship to the thing they are supposedly buying, doesn't always translate into a student experience of wanting to be there in the classroom. For many students, college is just an extension of compulsory education: a prelude to wage labor through indenture. It doesn't help, of course, that many faculty replicate the authoritarian structures of the master and pupil, the hierarchy of grades and ranking, and the arbitrariness of deadlines. Despite the myth of the liberal arts as a freeing and creative pursuit that creates a well-rounded citizen, students often retain the attitude of being forced to be in a room for a certain amount of time, which I suppose is really the best preparation for a job. The pity is this resistance to the situation doesn't typically transform into outright rebellion. There are teachers who style themselves as radical educators, still lodged within the institution, trying to provide space for study against the norms. Though many of these educators still buy into a certain degree to the narratives of responsibility, development, and work that cover over the darker racial-colonial side of education.

The other distinctions that start being drawn in the education system are between the normal and the other, modeling the right kind of self and the upright citizen. Not only do the systems of racism, masculine domination, and heterosexual normalization, ideas of citizenship, belonging, nation, and the state, and even concepts of correct political action get instilled in our brains in school. School also instills in us a self-conception, an identity, and an individualism, through competition and the processes of socialization that tend to include heavy bullying, and through the promotion of a correct pathway through life if you are to rise in society's ranks. At the same time that students learn of the progressive achievements of freedom by liberal nation states, they will experience the naturalization of hierarchical differences in the amount of access, the kind of attention, and the racialized, gendered division of the student body.

However, in our continuous anarchist attempt to denaturalize the things in our life that we take for granted, and to break up with the forms that don't serve us, we have to see that even the process of becoming human is a process of indoctrination. Whatever "natural" impulses we might have as creatures are never accessed purely and simply outside of the stories we tell about our lives. And here, I don't mean natural impulses in terms of "animal instinct," but rather our impulses to collaborate and create a world that prioritizes life and joy. Much of Western civilization is built on the denial of these impulses. School works to frame our impulses within the overarching ideology of our culture: punishing some, vaunting others. In fact, education is a training in naturalization of our differences into particular identities that we then discover and use to express ourselves through our life choices (i.e. jobs).

Anarchist Study

We can think of anarchism within Meyerhoff's framework as a particular mode of study, which aims to build a world without enshrined hierarchies, enforced domination, and coerced participation. Applying this to our relationship to education, we can see anarchist study as a lens through which we receive different forms of knowledge and evaluate them based on their relationship of power: to what extent does this reaffirm an entrenched system of hierarchy, like capital, the state, race, gender, and so on? How can I study this otherwise, in a way that promotes collective freedom? This approach is why I think of anarchism, in our current situation, as providing a mode of study that on one hand denaturalizes the things we are taught to think of as eternal, unchanging, essential, biological, and sedimented. This "negative" side of an anarchist relation to education—the disentanglement it might provide from education as a cultural process of normalizing the hierarchies that dominate our life—can lead to positive discoveries. It can help us to orient ourselves within the world of hierarchies, violence, and state power and reframe our approaches to promote collective liberation. That is, it helps us be less duped by the subtle forms of control that come in the form of entertainment, media, public discourse, and family cultures.

Therefore, on the other hand—a more "positive" side—we can focus on an anarchist "world-making and study," to see how our modes of study are a fundamental part of building the world we want to inhabit together. The education system and its profitable economic entanglements are the outgrowth of colonial European modes of study, which have enshrined racial hierarchies through universalized and seemingly neutral scientific ideas, and which also combine with and contribute to the machinery of capitalism. We only need to look to histories of resistant study to see that there are ongoing and historical examples of learning and world-building constantly pushed out of focus—often through romanticized notions of their "pastness." There is extensive work by Indigenous thinkers like Leanne Betasamosake Simpson on the way Indigenous modes of study are integrated with human and more than human inhabitants and the land, practicing and embodying the norms of their world, as a mutual experience of communication. We can also point to the Black radical tradition. Fred Moten and Stefano Harney's influential book, *The Undercommons,* poses as an "exit strategy for Black study," which includes Black knowledge and world-making within and against institutions like the university, but also study in typically unconsidered places such as the dinner table, song lyrics, the patterns of everyday speech, and more. For them, study can happen in schools but cannot be contained there. And the act of distinguishing what counts as knowledge (or learning) repeats the power distinctions we are trying to undo. Their position goes against a dichotomy of for or against schools. As I discussed in relation to work, while these institutions exist, we can think of them as places to enter and redistribute access and resources.

The undercommons theorizes a way of working on the inside and the outside—breaching that distinction that school tries to instill. There is a general consensus that the school itself, as instituted by state and corporate interests, cannot be a site of liberation. But it can be stolen from, like we discussed in the context of work in Chapter 3, and it can be used as a site of connection and distribution. And, following Meyerhoff, we can use these tools to enable a mode of study that would lead to the destruction of schooling and education and the building of other worlds of liberation.

The negative and positive have to go hand in hand. We need to unlearn the dominant systems and ways of thinking that naturalize hierarchies of race, gender, sexuality, and class. But then we can expand our understanding of study to our communities, to the act of care for each other, for our surrounding land, and for the creatures we cohabit the earth with. If you untangle normative education systems, and even the history of knowledge produced by the West, you start to realize that many of our basic concepts are grounded in the same processes that produced colonialism, racism, white supremacy, patriarchy, and capitalism—right down to our understanding of the human, of civilization, and of our place in the world. The expansion of study allows those structures to founder on the alternative production of knowledge through experience in the world, in community, and in process.

What's at Stake in Anarchist Study?

That the space of study also contains seeds of danger for the power system can be seen in the so-called culture wars carried out by the reactionary right over decades. At the same time that education is held up as a democratic right, and there is an ideology of unrestricted and uncensored access to knowledge, there is really strict control over what can be taught and how it can be taught. School is a bogeyman of the right because they see it as a hot bed of radical thinking, since ultimately there is a freedom in reading and thinking. And they are right, to a degree. In the end, what goes on inside a person's head cannot be fully monitored or controlled, but that most often happens in resistance to what one has access to in school. While it is possible to learn something other than dominant narratives in school, it is not assured or even likely. That is why study towards liberation would need to be supplemented.

There have been many theories of pedagogy that try to reframe institutional learning in a student-centered direction, including various attempts at anarchist schools and learning spaces. I won't rehearse all the different approaches that try to counteract the routines and disciplinary function of school and to loosen the hold of a standardized curriculum on the curiosity and interest of students. One of the tricky things to balance in a formal learning setting is the needs of an individual with the needs of a group, which is one of the main tensions that anarchism has to deal with: how to square autonomy with community. People have different learning styles, as well as different interests that they might want to follow. Self-directed learning thus would be an essential ingredient of an anarchist education, allowing people to follow their curiosities and talents. But group study is important too, not only for the way it opens one up to the ideas of others and the unexpected connections that can come from that, but also for the way that it helps us figure out how best to interact towards shared aims—in other words, building the world we want. Additionally, collaborative study helps undo the individualist mentality that schools instill, with competition for grades and honors.

Self-directed study allows people to determine what they want to pursue, based on their interests, but is limited to the contingency of knowledge and ideas made available to them and through the skills they develop. To hold that in tandem with a group pursuing work together, whether it involves presenting ideas as a way of sharing discoveries or interrogating ideas together, creates a necessary instance of communal study, a form of experimenting with ideas through feedback and discussion. The reason homeschooling can go so wrong is that it can create an echo chamber of uninterrogated ideas (for example, the dominant form of homeschooling in the USA involves Christian fundamentalist reactionary attempts to keep children from learning anything contrary to their beliefs). Of course, this idea could be leveled at anarchist approaches to learning as a form of anti-state indoctrination. But anarchism as I am presenting it here works not as a specific content of knowledge but rather as an opening up to multiple ways of living and different emphases on what is important for life, all existing side by side without enforcing dominance or erasure. An anarchist study would break down the hierarchies that education imposes in order to create the conditions for this other world, a prefiguration which leave room for experimentation. We don't know where anarchism leads, but we can use it as a tool to reframe our relationship to ourselves, each other, and the world.

An anarchist curriculum would mean studying the actual histories of statecraft and capitalist enclosure, from the perspective of legacies of resistance. The consequences of this education tend to perform a radical shift in a person's vision of the world from what they had previously been seeing. There are parodies of this, like in the John Carpenter film *They Live*, where sunglasses allow the main character to see through all the advertising propaganda to the hidden forms of social control. But the storyline of Western democracy is such a compelling one, and the atrocities are often distanced so well from our collective imaginations, that people can easily be duped into believing in the myth of the progressive arc of history: that we know better now, that we will continually and naturally do better, and that brutality is in the past or a characteristic of insufficiently modernized people. This narrative exempts us all from acting immediately to make things better now, and narrows our understanding of what legitimate action is. It also neglects the glaring fact that modernity has been a history of unflinching violence, specifically against people that do not fit within the cis straight white able-bodied norms.

Anarchism Is Perpetual Study

The version of anarchism that I am suggesting here counteracts the progress narrative completely, to the extent that anarchism can extricate itself from this kind of triumphalist linear thinking. Anarchism isn't a thing we achieve if we work hard enough. It's a way of living and relating right now. If we disconnect from the storylines that we are taught in school, we open up for investigation all the space in the past and the present (and the future) that operate outside or against of surveillance, control, and authority. This approach includes carving out those spaces within the current institutions, to the extent that we can, from which we can provide care and support to others and launch attacks against the powers that try to dominate us; no matter how fleeting these spaces are.

The enclosed form of education that occurs primarily through schooling displaced other forms of training and study that occurred through practice. Anarchism might pick up an apprenticeship approach but perhaps while rejecting the idea of mastery. Learning a skill from someone who does that skill (skillfully) is the opposition to the professionalization of knowledge that determines one, often costly, approach to learning how to do something. The professionalization of different skills tends to include licensing, which brings the state into the regulation of the skill and its availability. Our current education system relies on specialized knowledge, credentials of professionalism, and a certain pathway of proving your competency in these ideas. Part of the work of the state (and capital) is to teach us to be dependent on them for our survival, even if help is never actually forthcoming. This dependency grows not only through increasing our distance from knowing how to reproduce ourselves (any kind of knowledge of subsistence, for example, while gardening is a cute hobby), but also through regulations like licensure and safeguarding of knowledge access, intellectual property, and the general bureaucracy we are trained to navigate in getting access to anything. On the other hand, mentorship could be seen as a way of forming community bonds and solidarity in sharing resources of knowledge through direct passing on, outside any institutional control. Apprentice–mentor relationships set up gifts of knowledge from one person to the next and create a space in which innovation can be shared. Finally, this study is based in experience and grounds practice in action, rather than creating the divide of school and the real world that so many students feel they have to cross after graduation.

The constant emphasis on STEM (science, technology, engineering, and mathematics) education in today's culture aims to train servants to the current technocratic, militarized, industrialized state. However, in the light of the progress narrative, STEM learning gets played up through the liberal diversity schemes of increasing representation of women or Black people in science and tech fields. Despite the aim of inclusion, this process contributes to the siloing off of knowledge from an integrated relationship to our lives. The emphasis on innovation, plus a weighting of certain forms of knowledge as more important (practical, profitable) than others, further entrenches our understanding of study as an individualist endeavor ultimately tied to our goal to be successful, that is, to make as much money as possible.

The emphasis on science and technology creates a distinction between practical knowledge (the kind that is used to make things that supposedly help our lives) and impractical knowledge (e.g. an understanding of history or art). This distinction might not seem so nefarious, but consider that this shifts our attention away from understanding the ideological, political, social, and economic structure of our world, and brings our attention to an assumed transparent apolitical truth of the way the world works (i.e. a certain view of science). Science is easily taken out of the social-political context of discovery and deemed a universal good, despite the ways that it ties in with military industrial development and the continued imposition of Western ways of life on the world at large. The preference for science and technology helps naturalize the technocratic aspect of the ordering of our lives through the state, where policy experts determine the possibilities of life separate from our own ability to decide autonomously what matters to us. Thus, it ultimately contributes to the narrowing of politics to the electoral spectacle, while the nitty-gritty is left in the hands of trained functionaries.

So much of our education conditions us not to trust our own experiences and thereby makes many possibilities of experience invisible to us. Just like the lifelong tutelage of capitalism and the state trains us to think there is no viable life outside of their confines (despite the fact, as this book tries to show, that so much of what actually gets done contradicts that), we get trained to accept what is deemed knowledge and what is valued, right down to our senses, so that we don't even perceive things that don't fit into the accepted worldview. Perhaps the most practical knowledge we have is embodied in our interdependence: the way we learn to care for each other and ourselves in our communities. Not only does this care work get invisibilized because it is gendered as women's work, it is also taken out of the category of study, though it is fundamentally the mode in which we live. The anarchist idea of study and world-building would break down the boundaries of enclosure to see our engagement with our surrounding as continual learning, an ongoing dialogue, something we can take great care in and which changes moment to moment as the surroundings shift.

Does Study Lead to Freedom?

But is liberation dependent on a certain kind of study? We can probably trace this understanding back to the ideology of the Enlightenment, which posited itself as a progressive history of demolishing superstition and furthering human control over the earth. It has been used as a tactic in various movements for freedom. But this terrain of confrontation still belongs to the power system, through a process of assimilation into the normative structure that education tries to obtain by deciding what is inside and outside. Anarchist study will eventually have to untangle the ways that knowledge has been used to shore up the power systems that have been translated into our understandings of race, gender, sexuality, and hierarchy in general. I see this as a lifelong process of individual and collective work that we then turn into practice through not reproducing those forms of discipline and control.

The alternative approach, then, would imagine study as a process of reading, of interpreting the world, rather than knowledge as an object to be gained (and owned like property), that is, form over content. Matching our refrain of anarchist disidentification and dissolution, study moves through things, it does not hold on to them. Study favors collaboration and aims whatever it produces (in forms of knowledge and other resources) towards undoing these hierarchies and the sense of their innateness. Study is world-building and care. It cannot be enclosed, since it is our basic relationship to our environment. Study is capacious and all forms of life can apply.

We always study in collaboration, whether we are reading the work of someone who has woven together ideas from their own research, or whether we are actively studying alongside others to transform our world through ideas we create together. In school, we are rewarded for individual endeavor, and we are expected to make "unique contributions" to the fields we study. And yet, all of our so-called knowledge (giving it the possessive, like we contain and own it, is inaccurate) is built on combined work. As a person who studies literature, I understand all texts to be made up of "a tissue of quotations," as Roland Barthes describes it in "The Death of the Author." And so all the contributions we make could be figured like sampling in music, the mashing up of influences, juxtaposing ideas to create new instances of understanding. All study, too, has to be provisional, pending, and ready to be dismissed. As an ideology, anarchism works this way: not professing an end goal (say communism) but demanding continual attention, as Ursula K. Le Guin's anarchist scientist realizes in the novel *The Dispossessed*, so that our organizations don't calcify and end up blocking learning, collaboration, or joy. Thus our embodied anarchism is a lifelong apprenticeship in community with other people, since it requires us to warn against power inhering in an abusive way while experimenting with better ways to relate to each other and the world around us. Anarchism is a perpetual course correction. It leaps into the unknown, scales falling from the eyes, demanding a future that can't be predicted.

FAQs

Isn't education one of the most important things we can invest in?

We can't separate learning from the context in which it happens. While we pick up important skills in school, the institution itself works to mold our thinking in line with the logic of the state and capital. For one thing, the process of schooling literally breaks our body into the mold of regimented time for work. Little children don't want to sit in rooms all day. Teenagers don't want to wake up first thing in the morning to rush to school. School instills competition and false ideas of meritocracy, and naturalizes hierarchical differences like race and gender. Imagine studying in a variety of other contexts on your own time, with your own energy, in collaboration, without false objective evaluation. We might also think about how educational processes sever us from our environment, which would then allow us to rethink study as integration with the world around us, not mastery over it through knowledge.

Isn't all schooling propaganda?

Anarchism sees study as a world-making endeavor, so in a way, the answer would be "yes." But, while educational institutions instill the culture of the surrounding power system, an anarchist approach to study would promote ways of being and relating that allow a society of autonomy and mutual responsibility. We typically use the word propaganda to refer to totalitarian attempts to control behavior through messaging—it's a version of ideology, a description of the world that mystifies the true power relations. Anarchism might engage in propaganda but not through mystification. Connecting people with their own power—individually and collectively—allows for self-determination rather than conformity.

5

How Do We Pay for It? Anarchy in Your Wallet and in the Market

- We can't save or spend our way to freedom
- Money isn't real, but it steals our lives
- Let's get enough for us all to survive

Anarchism and the Economy

Anarchists will debate among themselves, and with other libertarian anti-authoritarian tendencies, whether we can have a society with money that doesn't enforce hierarchy, whether we ought to exchange goods through something like a market, and then what kind of lives we want to be living, what kinds of things we think we will need, and how we will share resources to make and distribute those things. How much industrial and technological development do we want to retain and reframe on liberatory lines? How do people share products made in different geographical areas based on different available resources? How do we circulate goods among loosely federated autonomous societies? Revolutionary thinking often gets caught in trying to maintain the content of our current lives under capitalism, just without capitalists. Typically this ends up reasserting the need for a centralized state to oversee distribution.

There are many like-minded projects that people undertake in order to actively construct alternative ways of organizing our lives outside of the economy. Different communities develop their own currency that isn't issued by the state and therefore form a different mutual type of exchange outside of the relation to capital. Communities might even form their own banks to share resources for different projects. Similarly, in *Anarchism and the Black Revolution*, Lorenzo Kom'boa Ervin takes the term "dual power" to describe the kind of world-building we can undertake that meets our current needs and forms a point of resistance to the state. The Malcolm X Grassroots Movement takes the term "solidarity economics" from Latin American social movements of the 1980s and 1990s, as well as the Mondragon Corporation in Spain, to describe the vision they support: in Cooperation Jackson in Mississippi people are trying to build food autonomy, provide housing access, and engage in participatory budgets to direct state and municipal funding to their projects. One method people might engage in is turning workplaces into worker-owned cooperatives, or forming community land trusts to wrest property from state or corporate ownership. All of these ideas engage in some way with the current economy towards a transformation of it. The idea is to find the cracks of the system and try to widen them.

The Meaning of Money

Money might be a privileged space for us to examine the ways we invest meaning in things through the hope that their value will persist. Like the state and capitalism, money is naturalized: it is the medium of exchange, something eternal and life-defining, even if it is simultaneously derided and worshiped. Can we relate to money without investing in its future? Can we disconnect ourselves from the ethereal rule it has over our lives? This isn't to disregard the very real fact that our material lives and existence are often dependent on having enough money to buy the products we need to survive. But demystifying money—disidentifying from its power—may help free up our wallets. We might find survival, even thriving, in other informal ways of sharing, if we don't individualize our need for food, shelter, and other objects but make it a communal concern.

For one thing, money isn't real. By this I don't mean that it doesn't have real material effects in our world. But as we can see in the financialization of markets, most of the profits that are still being accumulated now are speculative ventures and not tied to making anything that is used by anyone. It just exists to make more money. Those of us not engaged in these speculative ventures have no experience of money in this way, though most of us probably do have an experience of indebtedness, which is another aspect of the unreality of money (e.g. in the pandemic year, many people's student loans were put on hold, people didn't pay, and nothing changed due to that). Probably many of us have used credit to purchase necessities, hoping we'd later be able to cover that expense with future gain.

As Vicky Osterweil writes in *In Defense of Looting*, the process of forcibly integrating people into the money economy required the mass of people to "internalize" "the new economic and social relations developing," "to be forced to recognize the ways 'rational,' 'natural' ways of the new system of property, commodity, labor, and contract." All of these structures of the state (and market) require force, so that at the other end of this long history we have internalized most of these relations. At the beginning, the question was, as Osterweil writes, "[w]hat could the state do to keep these people paying rent and going to work and not, say, recognizing their own power, taking over society, and changing it in the interest of all?" The answer, she writes, developed into professionalized police forces: "transforming people into criminals is one of the core methods of social control under capitalism." I emphasize this point once again to bring out the fact that the social world we live in, which seems natural, inevitable, and unchangeable, has only come about through a long process of violent enforcement, with the police as the epitome of this violence.

Money itself is always covered in blood, and helps maintain the dominance of white supremacy, capitalism, and the state. W. E. B. DuBois wrote about the "wages of whiteness," as the extra benefit that poor white people were given in a racial hierarchy over Black people. But trace money back to the onset of industrial capitalism (or even back to mercantilism) and you see that the wealth of nations comes from genocide, capture, and enslavement, and thus played a significant role in creating the categories of race that we live with today, as well as the geopolitical distribution of power in which resources are extracted from (formerly) colonized areas and shuttled to the wealthy European-American countries. This is another reason for us to shift our relationship to money, to break ourselves out of the cycle of need and want and struggle to survive, towards a struggle for something else: to let what money we do have change hands with other people who need it too, especially those with less access.

The False Moralism of Money

The relationship to money in Western society that is dominant tends to entail some form of moralism, whether it's the shaming of people without resources for not having anything or the vaunting of those selfish enough to base their lives on exploiting others for their own gain.

While money—having it, not having it, saving it, spending it—carries moral weight, capitalism poses itself as an amoral or neutral ideology that is simply the best way to organize an economy. It therefore naturalizes money as the means of exchange and the goal of survival. And the state and capital work together to posit an essential divide between politics and economics, so that we can imagine that economics is a science with laws that are beyond us, though it is really created through our actions and imposed on us by the state, its institutions, and the owners. The reality is that the financial system we've inherited and are forcibly inserted into is the result of years of blood and theft, of settler/colonialism, of racialized slavery and hierarchies. Just as people like to say there is no ethical consumption under capitalism, we might add that there is no such thing as clean money. There's no job that pays you from a source that isn't tainted, there are no savings that aren't dependent upon markets that kill, there's no clean way to earn or spend.

We know from experience that money can't buy us happiness, but it is still necessary for survival. We might be able to disentangle ourselves from its overdetermined moralism: the kind that finds money itself simply evil and or equates financial worth with one's moral worth.

Money can be "invested" with so much meaning because ultimately it is an empty reference, an item of exchange that abstractly assigns equivalencies, especially after currency was removed from the gold standard and no longer even refers to a material object deemed valuable.

(Though, even the "gold standard" was an arbitrary assignment of value and has a history intertwined with colonialism and genocide.) In other words, money's actual abstraction allows it to bear all manner of connotations.

Yet, by the very fact that we are forced to earn it and spend it to survive, it's incredibly hard to see it clearly. In the spirit of disidentification, then, I suggest we track down all the ways we naturalize money and its apparent moral value in our lives. The idea that time is money enforces our waged labor. Boycotting or buying local or fair trade may be no more than another consumer identity trying to express our moral preferences without direct actions. If we acknowledge that spending or not spending money is not going to make or break the revolution, we can free up space to disinvest from the relations to power that money normalizes for us—that is, including even the moralistic idea that we can make a clean individual break with it.

The Myth of the Moral Consumer

A popular activist tactic that seems perfectly aimed at capitalism is the boycott. Famously, this tactic worked during the Montgomery bus boycott of 1955–6, legendarily kicked off by Rosa Parks' refusal to move to the back of the bus. Similar to the method employed by the strike, where workers stop production (turn labor time to zero), the consumer refuses to purchase. Since the Montgomery bus boycott and the co-optation of the Black liberation movement in the USA into the narrative of civil rights as an accomplished fact, the tactic of boycott has transformed into a more liberal individual act divorced from movement building or direct action. Thus, we might appraise the apparent non-participation in the market as a more reform-oriented attempt to affect the market enough to demand concessions, which ultimately doesn't threaten the market itself. Though it can achieve some results, and is part of a larger repertoire of tactics—for example the Palestinian Boycott, Divestment, and Sanctions movement that targets support for Israel along several lines, including companies and academic institutions—it also risks tying into an individualist consumer moralism that gets used to co-opt movement energy.

In the wake of the famous wielding of boycotts in the civil rights movements, and the increasing concentration of production into global megacorporations, we see brands become more savvy about their image to avoid being tarnished by bad press and to help whitewash their actual production practices. A simple call out on social media about the apparent racism or homophobia or misogyny in an advertisement can suffice to get an apology, and then a new ad campaign that includes the discourse of the resistant group as a selling point. Boycotts can therefore easily be captured by the workings of the market.

Similarly, much of the response to the global climate catastrophe, in part caused by processes like clear cutting and the overproduction of meat, has been individualized through a moralizing of consumer choice. At the grocery store, we are encouraged to bring reusable bags. We are shamed for plastic water bottles. None of these considerations hit at the point of production or social organization at large. It shies away from demanding why water might be bottled and sold, rather than made freely accessible in healthy ways.

All of this moralizing operates under the false assumption that our individual choices have the power to shift the tide towards a greener future, without indicting the corporations and the states that support them for their massive projects of resource extraction and production of waste. Our individual buying habits don't cause the desertification of the planet. Likewise, it is a fallacious argument to say that consumer demand creates these markets, since we are actually limited in our options of what we can buy, not only based on what we can afford but on the corporations' ever-present interest of increasing profits to the detriment of any other consideration.

We can make whatever choices we want at the supermarket without really making any significant change in the overall scheme of things. The effectiveness of boycotts relies on a mass demonstration of refusal, and that massive movement doesn't currently exist. Therefore, we might take a different approach than the traditional idea of massive politics and mass movements while also trying to avoid the pitfalls of the idea of a vanguard party leading the way to liberation. Just as capitalism and the state have developed unevenly and differently in different contexts, our refusals might be unevenly spread and only through repetition and coordination build into larger actions.

To be sure, this tends to approach revolution in a somewhat individualist way, by talking about the things we can do in our day-to-day lives to alter our vision of the world we inhabit, in order to help us disidentify with the structure of the world as it is. But the individual work we do to disidentify actually opens us up to a collectivity only previously experienced in glimpses, creating possibilities for different arrangements that bring us together. In other words, delinking our individual standpoints from the ingrained logics of state, market, and hierarchy utterly changes the terrain of group action. We are so often trapped in an idea of identity that turns the things you like and do into an eternal rule of your being: I'm a hunting man, a soccer mom, a punk, a goth, a jock, etc. It's that pernicious individualism we want to dislodge. Here, we disrobe ourselves from the need to be one thing so that we can be multiple, together; reshaping our lives in ideas of collective care, relationships, and world-building.

No Future, Just Now

Reframing our understanding of money won't disentangle us from needing it to survive, but it can free us up to use it differently and also to seek out forms of exchange outside of the money economy. One major way we can approach this disidentification is by counteracting the future orientation of saving up for a life we may never even reach. If we think about what we have and need in the moment, we can see what is extra, and therefore what we can share with the people around us in need—whether it's someone we randomly meet or a friend who we know is struggling. This relationship to others is the fundamental anarchist idea of mutual aid, and money, like other resources, can also serve us as a form of cooperation in the moment.

Capitalism always orients us to the future, and this gets replicated in our basic political forms as well as our entire lives (since really none of these things are easy to separate). As we are daily striving to get by, we are looking towards an ever uncertain future. The state plays on our sense of fear, to keep us working for the minimal scraps we get, rather than refusing and withdrawing. It is hard to think about radical change now or in the future, when the ground we stand on feels like it could be ripped out at any time. (Incidentally, this dynamic is a hallmark of abusive relationships as well, where the abuser keeps the person they are abusing on their toes, never settled in a comfortable position.)

The rhetoric of capitalism for workers insists that saving money correctly will allow them to buy the kind of social mobility they are assumed to be chasing: first and foremost, owning a home, since property consolidates wealth. Of course, this idea about how a poor person should save instead of spend doesn't take into account all the bills and debts that pile up just trying to survive, from healthcare to rent to tax to credit cards that try to bridge the gap of low wages and high prices. Meanwhile, rich people can stockpile money, and they don't have to pay the same kind of taxes, they get things handed to them for free, and they live lives that are less prone to complete upheaval based on a single unpredictable event like an accident, a traffic ticket, or a layoff.

Orienting ourselves towards our future comfort—like the idea of retirement, a time when things will be easier if only we work hard enough—forces us to keep repeating the present conditions that keep us in check. It binds away our time and energy from actively resisting, while also helping enable not only the mindset but the actual material reality of the majority of people who are in precarious situations struggling to survive and feeling lucky to get even minimal compensation. All of our money goes into the marketplace, supporting this structure: landlords, debt collectors, corporations, the city, county, state, and country. The stress of living under these conditions also affects our health, making it uncertain that we will ever reach this future of retirement, after work, where we can actually enjoy life. In this way, capitalism operates an endless deferral of the real life we want—except in the way we consume it through media, watching the lives of the privileged in sitcoms, movies, and reality TV. Let's reject the future of improbable wealth and recount what we have right now. Our daily lives deserve more of our attention, because ultimately it is in these moments and the relationships that sustain us that we continue to make or transform the power dynamics. If we have the money in our pocket, which of us has a need that can be met right now?

Forge Bonds, Don't Buy Them

Money as the medium of exchange relieves the necessity of human relationship in the process of exchange. Buying is a totally impersonal procedure, even more so as small stores get swallowed by big chains: I go to the store, pick the thing I want, hand over some cash or charge it to a card, and leave. No one I deal with has any interest in the actual exchange; they are merely paid to service it. If I need to return the item, there are rules for that and I'm reimbursed. The seller has no claim on it, it's over. If I resell it, that's my choice. In fact, this mindset infects most of the ways we relate to the world—it is even imbedded in the policing function and is the main way the state operates. We want to relinquish responsibility, we want an authority to handle any problems—these are all intermediaries to conflict resolution. We don't even need to be grounded in any particular location, we move on when our opportunities cease in any one spot.

Again, at the bottom of money's nefarious effect on us is the issue of care and relationships. One major way for us to rethink our relationship to each other—and to money—would be to think about how it can be used against purposes, to forge bonds rather than to pay off our responsibility. An alternative economic thinking that many anarchists refer to is "the gift economy." The conceptualization of this comes from the French sociologist (and revolutionary socialist) Marcel Mauss's 1925 book *Essay on the Gift*. David Graeber frames Mauss's ideas through an anarchist lens in *Fragments of an Anarchist Anthropology*:

> Before Mauss, the universal assumption had been that economies without money or markets had operated by means of "barter"; they were trying to engage in market behavior (acquire useful goods and services at the least cost to themselves, get rich if possible ...), they

just hadn't yet developed very sophisticated ways of going about it. Mauss demonstrated that in fact, such economies were really "gift economies." They were not based on calculation, but on a refusal to calculate; they were rooted in an ethical system which consciously rejected most of what we would consider the basic principles of economics. It was not that they had not yet learned to seek profit through the most efficient means. They would have found the very premise that the point of an economic transaction—at least, one with someone who was not your enemy—was to seek the greatest profit deeply offensive.

Mauss's picture demonstrates that people can also operate outside of the calculation of profit and individual benefit. But this is something we all know, as we have likely given gifts to our loved ones not out of obligation or for a holiday but simply because we could. Like many counternarratives to the dominant story, Mauss's demonstration that modern economies aren't traced back to barter is rejected in favor of a progressivist or false evolutionary narrative that justifies the imposition of capitalist markets as an innate human feature finally realized. If we hold the relationship of the gift in mind, we can see that there are ways to maintain other forms of exchange at the same time that we are forced to operate in a capitalist money economy. No method of exchange is natural—they are held up through custom or, as we have seen in the case of capitalism, enforced by other means.

The gift ostensibly creates a space for you within a community, through a sort of obligation. Or more accurately, the gift creates the social relations of obligation to one another. It reframes our understanding of reciprocity, which is the supposed foundation of something like barter or the assignation of value with money: I give you this for that, and it's fair. The gift doesn't claim equal return but rather demands an obligation of a further gift (usually with the aim to outdo the previous gift). To reframe it in an ethical way, it promotes the desire to give and share and create a world together, outside of property. And yet, the gift brings us into a series of exchanges that are given a different note than capitalist exchange: I give you something I have, you give me something you have. They aren't equal or even contemporaneous. Anarchism ima-gines a freedom that isn't divested from mutual responsibility.

The French thinker Georges Bataille thinks of the gift as a way to refute concepts of "utility" and the logic or rationality that is used to support economic thinking. In fact, he claims, the gift is traced to waste, towards a spending without reserve—something that gets distorted in the capitalist relationship through untouchable luxuries and ultimately, he argues, in the bourgeoisie's wasting of the proletariat. I find this a compelling way of considering gift giving because it also allows us a dif-ferent relationship to "luxury," which seems so inextricably linked with consumer culture. An anarchist relationship to money, then, would be a wanton spending of whatever you have on everything and anyone. Therefore spending could even run parallel to something like looting, where people refuse to pay for the things they need—or the things they want. Money is destructive and is based in its own theft—of our time and our own lives. We can embody this destruction and stealing for our own ends. I'd like to extend this idea of luxury in terms of what is unaccounted for: our luxury exceeds accounting, exceeds reciprocity, exceeds reason, exceeds profit, exceeds perhaps even visibility. Luxury might be staring into space daydreaming. The other side of productivity isn't simply destruction but unexchangeable time: our lives.

Meetings Needs and Needing More

Short of burning our money, though, how does this perspective help us think about spending our few resources? There are different approaches that merge the market non-participation of boycott with the giving of gifts, but which are aimed at fulfilling our needs and desires rather than a reformed market integration. An anarchist tradition is the "Really Really Free Market," a dig at the fact that the supposed "free market" of capitalism actually needs the state to enforce it and prop it up. The anar-chist free market is free in that no money is needed. Everyone comes with the stuff they want to give, and anyone can leave with the things they want or need. No questions asked. It's a temporary, scheduled point of mutual aid, where people plan to come together with the resources and possessions they don't need, to offer them up to anyone who wants to take them. The free store is a version of mutual aid, although one that is not developed in a pressing crisis (e.g. in relation to environmental catastrophe, or the pandemic, or even around street movements) but in daily life outside extraordinary difficulties (though daily life is difficult enough). The free store creates a community situation where people come together to get their needs met outside of the money economy and the hierarchies it creates, just for everyday living. It is a concrete redistribution of resources.

The counterpoint that always comes up in situations like this is: how do we regulate someone taking more than they need? Of course, someone might always ruin the party. The main tendency, however, is actually the opposite: people tend to avoid "conspicuous consumption" since we have been moralized away from our pleasure in things. But there are a few possible responses to the possibility of someone exploiting the generosity: first of all, maybe that person needs the indulgence. Though if it became a habit of taking too much, it would just point to our responsibility to talk with each other, to figure out how to share in a way that feels better. The worst case scenario would be that the person is unwelcome in the space. If someone is doing something that feels harmful, why not address it directly and autonomously? We tend to sit and judge people for doing things we disapprove of, trained as we are to only bring in third parties to regulate apparent disorder, when we could simply start a conversation. The issue may not be resolved in a satisfying way, but these are the risks we need to take in order to determine things for ourselves. While money divests us from responsibility for anything that happens outside of the exchange, the free store makes us face the complexity of our relationships.

Now, redistribution poses another problem. In queer anarchist circles, for example, we often tend to redistribute our own limited funds among ourselves, passing the same dollar around to help each other pay for things we need, whether it's gender-affirming surgery, hormones, or rent. It's not a top-down redistribution but sort of like passing around the same dollar to everyone. Certainly, we can reframe our relationship to our access to money through fulfilling our basic needs and then distributing the rest. If you have access to a regular salaried income, it's very easy to budget for your needs and then commit the extra to other things. It's also important to question what your actual needs are in the moment, to live outside, as far as we can, the constant fear of losing everything or, perhaps more accurately, outside of the moralism of saving.

We can delink our ideas of ownership from money—it's not yours, it's merely a current medium of exchange that people are forced to use to get their basic needs. Incidentally, the people with less money are more prone to help each other out, despite the fact that rich people have more money, since they hoard it away. Meanwhile, poor people have to spend whatever little they have—and still find ways to have luxury, enjoyment, and dangerous pleasure. Gifts, waste, and luxury help us think outside scarcity and its mentality. If we displace the moralism of money as the sign of individual worth and hard work into an ethics of relationship that fosters connection and shared meeting of needs, we can alter our relationship to the thing that marks so much of our lives.

Take All You Can Get and Share Whatever You Have

So if capitalism programs us to look always to the future, while we barely breathe in the present, our way to resist that in the realm of money is to refuse that orientation. We have to shrug off all of the moralism that money is imbued with, along with all of the shame that comes with not having money and needing help. If the state offers us any resources, we should take them. There is no shame in claiming unemployment benefit or receiving food stamps. We can't accept the narrative that says receiving help makes you dependent, as if dependence is a bad thing. As the disability justice movement has taught, the reality we live in is one of interdependence. No one can be fully self-sufficient.

Still, if we get more than we need, we redistribute. Similar to the relationship to workplace resources, we can steal from the state to give to people in need. When we do have cash on hand, we can try to remove our mindset from the fear of not having money tomorrow, next week, or next year, and share what we do have with the people in our communities that need a little help right now. It seems small and insignificant, but relating to money differently in this way, not as a scarce resource to hoard jealously against anyone else's use or to save in a bank until a big purchase can be made, helps deprogram us from its stranglehold on our consciousness. As glo merriweather has taught, you aren't paying your rent, or that bill today, but in the future. Now, you have the money in your pocket—can you share it? Another way, perhaps, to think of this—for we are living in a time of ongoing and worsening climate catastrophe—is to question ourselves on what we are saving for? What future will come? Certainly not one that looks anything like the present we live in now, and not at all like the one earlier generations experienced. In fact, the future we want can't look like the world right now—we refuse to reproduce it by saving for a life that we can't even reach. Even though people without money get caught in the grind of always trying to get more, we also know that having money itself is only temporary, and therefore we should use it.

But to end on a more tangible note, we can always return to the time-tested anarchist action of stealing. In *Riot. Strike. Riot*, Clover argues that looting performs "negation of market exchange and market logic," and in this lies its ethical value: "Looting is not the moment of falsehood but of truth echoing across centuries of riot: a version of price-setting in the marketplace, albeit at price zero. It is a desperate turn to the question of reproduction, though one dramatically limited by the structure of capital within which it initially operates." In other words, looting doesn't break us out of capitalism, but it does break us from the policing structure of consumption and production and exchange through money. Clover claims the goods still have a price, even if that price is zero. But this redistribution in its destruction could be prefigurative of a place and time where we share what we have: everything for everyone, as the slogan goes. If property is theft, we could see our ethical duty as stealing back what really is ours, or rather, it belongs to no one, we only use it for a moment—not just necessities but also luxuries. (These always get criticized in riots, when people steal TVs or expensive clothes.) Contrary to the media representation, during a riot people looting tend to take care of each other and help everyone get what they need or want. It's not the same individualized endeavor as shopping.

So even in the store, why not take what we can? We internalize the police function, thinking this doesn't belong to us. We even get the small business ethos drilled into our head: shop local. And yet, we might ask if these businesses pay their employees well? What do they give to us that we should give to them? In addition to the "Great Refusal" of people to go back to work in the Covid-19 pandemic, there has also been a phenomenon of coordinated theft from chain stores, outside of the context of riots. It's a more mundane looting that doesn't require the more spectacular disorder that the riot produces. These people are already working around the need for money, and we can learn from that. There is no shame in stealing, from work, from the store—and there is even a more wonderful feeling of stealing a gift for someone else. Set the price at zero, save your money for someone else.

FAQs

Is there a right way to spend money?

Liberals and certain leftists will impose a moralism of money and spending that does nothing to counter the dominance of capitalism over our lives. Through the money system, we are forced to engage in capitalism—we can't spend or not spend our way out of it. As long as we need money to get the bare necessities of life, we participate. Withholding our money can be powerful when coordinated. People can work towards things like food autonomy, for example, creating a community that doesn't rely on the global supply chains for subsistence. This would lead to a greater withdrawal from the economy—and pose a threat, probably big enough for state retaliation. In your area, you can also form alternative economies and exchanges that don't use the same dominant money system. However, in the current situation it is quite difficult to end participation. Of course, you can choose to spend your money where it goes more clearly towards workers—supporting collectively owned business. But access issues mean that most people are going to be spending their money at nefarious places. We can't demand purity in an imperfect world.

Am I allowed to buy things I want?

Again, we can't demand purity from ourselves when forced to participate in a bloody and compromised system. While I don't think wanton spending on desired objects spells freedom, I do favor using money when you have it for what you want and need rather than anxiously holding on to it for a rainy day—so many things intervene for workers to push the possibility of actual comfort further and further away, and those rainy days happen more and more frequently. You and your friends can pool your scant resources to splurge on luxury—use your food stamps for that expensive vegan ice cream (Government Bliss, as lore tells me the Portland anarchists called Coconut Bliss). Buy your friends a meal, bring some art into your life. Spend in ways that remind you our lives contain beauty and joy, not just bills and work.

6

Can We Still Enjoy Ourselves? Anarchy and Art

People sometimes inquire what form of government is most suitable
for an artist to live under. To this question there is only one answer.
The form of government that is most suitable to
the artist is no government at all.

Oscar Wilde, "The Soul of Man under Socialism"

- Art can both reproduce and counter the dominant world
- Art forms our desires and gives meaning to our daily lives
- Art can play an essential role in experimenting with different ways
  of living

Art and Revolution?

The question of art and revolution faces us with a seeming contradiction. We generally think of art as a place of creativity and imagination
that counters the norms of our world; and yet we also enshrine art as
the province of a select few—those with the "talent" (time and wealth)
to make it, not to mention those with the means to buy it. In our childhood, we may be encouraged to experiment with artistic forms, but soon
enough we are forced to "color inside the lines," and we lose our nerve
when we can't perfectly represent figures in our drawings. Later, we are
exposed to art through schooling as an obligatory process of encultur-
ation: trips to the museum to see the greats, a constructed situation
where you are supposed to have a particular experience of art, an experience that always feels elusive given the institutional setting. A distaste

no doubt emerges when we lose our own initiative, when we are forced to gaze upon an exclusive world from the outside, and when a hierarchy of good and bad (high and lowbrow) determines our taste. The most glaring critique is that high art is a market and wealth generator for the elite, while popular culture is a money-making scheme of corporations that feed us the myths of capitalism, the police, and the state.

But anarchists still cling to the liberatory possibilities of art: we make posters and patches and zines and performances. There are anarchist genres of music—historically punk has been a big part of contemporary anarchism, and there are ever more anarchist art collectives and printing workshops, all operating outside the institutional norms, with a DIY ethic in materials and distribution. Punk became fertile ground for an anarchist aesthetic since it was framed as an amateur genre, open to people regardless of skill or talent. Tearing down the walls between performer and audience, artist and viewer, author and reader, has long been a liberatory goal—at least in theory, even for the critics who still participate in the general high art world.

We can also use our anarchistic orientation to look critically at the most successful and popular art, with what bell hooks calls an "oppositional gaze." hooks notes that Black women watch movies knowing that they are typically not the prime audience, which creates the space for an oppositional reception of the work. We know that the art world is dominated by money, and that compromises many artists. And yet, we can use the art that inspires us to weave together parts and experiment with ideas that help us create visions of anarchy to empower us today and for tomorrow. We can make our own art that refuses to reproduce the world as it is, no matter whether it is figural or abstract. Art itself is its own terrain of struggle. Our engagement with cultural creations— whether we make them or enjoy them—becomes a major mode of us to disidentify, to try out our ideas of liberation, to question and experiment with different forms.

In Oscar Wilde's anarchist utopian vision of "The Soul of Man under Socialism," the abolition of private property would allow for each person to become an artist. However, in this world there would no longer be the great art that we know now, the province of the wealthy and fortunate:

living our lives and expressing our personality would be art in itself. The daily anarchism I propose in this book takes the cue from Wilde, so that a practical anarchism is itself a creative practice. We cannot give up that liberatory vision of creatively living in common. There have been more and more radical attempts to use different art forms, from music to image to narrative, to envision alternate possible worlds. Afrofuturist and Indigenous speculative fiction reframes the mainstream obsession with dystopian futures by showing that apocalypse has already happened, and is happening, for many—but the futures where Black and Indigenous people thrive are always being created now and again.

Our art doesn't have to be confined to traditional forms; as Wilde imagined, our lives are works of art. The practice of disidentifying and reorienting our relationships to others, to our place and time, through care and communication, is itself an art, a creative pursuit of something called living, which we have never actually known and is something we improvise as we go. As we look at modes of study outside of the process of schooling, we can rediscover the creative spark that norms dampen in us, so that we can permit ourselves to create in unrecognized or unrecognizable forms. We get sold typical trajectories of life that we must measure ourselves against, but we can experiment and play with our lives, knowing there is no single right way to live. I'm not here to say don't watch movies or TV—though we must imagine a world where corporations don't control all of our time. As anarchists, we don't want to completely remove ourselves from the dominant culture, but we can see how mainstream art reflects power to us. In our disidentification we can use anarchism as a frame of critique, just as we look at our own lives to root out the way we use power over other people. And in our anarchist reading of art, we can start to imagine other creative visions.

The Problem of Representation

[T]he game of representation, where they speak in the name of and in the place of the so-called totality about the results of an exploration they haven't even made.

Guy Hocquenghem, "Volutions"

Notions of identity give another layer of meaning to representation. Politically, it tends to play out as having people in power who share the identity markers of the people they wield power over—the people they allegedly represent. One less lethal way Black liberation movements were dismantled in the 1970s was through a wave of elections of Black mayors. But we see this push culturally too, in the methods of signaling diversity by tokenism: advertisements and TV shows that include a Black or Brown or gay or trans or X person in a supporting role. This cynical measure was particularly rife after the George Floyd uprising kicked off in earnest. Netflix, Amazon, etc. had their "Black Voices" or "Representation Matters" section, and movies representing Black liberation as spectacle were more and more available. In this case, diversity is an illusion, a representation that mirrors no actual world or that only amplifies representation of Black suffering.

Still, many people see representation as a potential means of liberation. Sure, there is an undeniably powerful feeling in finding people who share the same identity markers—we might just call them markers of systematic oppression—in unlikely places. It gives a sense that you are not alone in shouldering the burden, or that others survive and make it into places where they have been typically excluded. In another sense, the representation of difference through cultural production, such as movies, novels, poetry, plays, paintings, and other art forms, has been, at the least, a means of communication between the elites and the oppressed, if not a strong motor of progressivist, reformist change. It's true that narratives were a major tool in the early abolition movement, but they worked within the dehumanizing logic of settler colonialism and white supremacy. But the fact that we can try to locate liberation in representation, both politically and aesthetically, might already be symptomatic of the way that forms of power attempt to co-opt and dismantle our potential rebellion. In the 1960s, Guy Debord was already diagnosing capitalist modernity as "the society of the spectacle," another extension of Marx's idea of the commodity fetish, where our actual forms of living have been replaced by spectacle that we then consume as audience. In this view, our whole lives are inundated with representation, everything is fully mediated, and our lives are therefore alienated away from action. The Lettrists and then the Situationists practiced disruptions of the spectacle through détournement, which hijacked images and art from the dominant discourse to create oppositional ideas. This was part of the overall project of the Situationist International, to construct situations bridging art and life and to create spaces for more immediacy and action. The practice of détournement has lived on beyond the Situationist International, through the images of punk, culture jamming, and some political street art. But we may still ask whether motivating these images to liberation can't get captured again. The history of punk, for example, is tied to a history of fashion, and the subversion can be mass marketed.

There is clearly a connection between our political and cultural or aesthetic understandings of representation. Anarchists oppose deputizing power to a handful of elites through modern political systems of representation. Should we be equally suspicious of literary and visual forms of representation? We know that literature, movies, and so on do the work of ideology. Adorno and Horkheimer called this "the culture industry," producing items for consumption that obscured the difference between labor and leisure, training the consumer to perform the necessary tasks of exploitation. In fact, some of the most insidious tendrils of ideology are implanted in our minds through the narratives we are told incessantly from the beginning of our lives onward. Almost no one has had a positive interaction with the police, but in children's TV shows there is invariably a friendly neighborhood cop who is a part of the world in the show. And yet, despite the ways it reproduces ideology, literature and other representational art still entices us and promises subversion. Is there a way to play the game of representation on our own terms? Can we tell stories that fight power, that combat ideology, that point towards our collective liberation? How do we engage with the art and culture that surrounds us, as rebels?

The great cultural theorist Stuart Hall provides a helpful way for approaching our enmeshment with culture and the art, images, and ideas that circulate within it. Representation that circulates within the realm of culture does not, according to Hall, have a fixed or final meaning. Thus, representation itself becomes a terrain of struggle, not only in producing different art forms but also in our reception of them. Hall helps us identify different competing meetings within forms of representation, from the dominant meanings to resistant appropriations and interpretations. We don't need to be a passive audience to propaganda in the form of big budget films, sitcoms, advertisements, or even the news. And we also have to have a keen eye for the art that gets presented to us as progressive or either liberatory, for often it finds ways to recement the social order as inevitable, to present social and political conflicts as magically resolved, to pacify us into passively waiting for progress. Since the meaning is never fixed, and the representation itself is not transparent, there are always multiple interpretations. As anarchists, we disidentify with the hegemonic meaning, read against the grain, repurpose and take what we want, discarding or critiquing the rest. And perhaps, too, in our practice of disidentifcation, we must refuse the terms of art, whether as a consumer or practitioner, tearing down the walls that make it seem separate from our lives.

Against the Reality Principle

If the meaning of art and culture is a terrain of struggle, what is at stake? Often it's the very sense of reality itself. One of the main interventions our practical anarchism must make is in knowing that things don't have to be this way, that the dominant forms are not inevitable, and that, in fact, there are many differing worlds existing at the same time. Often the oppositional worlds get ignored, made invisible, left out of the narrative, which means we need storytellers to take up the task of retrieving counterhistories and alternative futures in their work. The dominance of realism as an aesthetic value is a major reason that art can be so disappointing politically. "Good" narrative art, as determined by academics and bourgeois critics, is often limited to works that reflect "reality." Even the experimental forms of novels tend to be understood as innovating a more accurate portrayal of reality. In narrative art like novels and films, this means replicating the "complex" and "adult" problems of middle-class cis-hetero families. This hegemony of realism leads to the distinction between realism and genres like science fiction and fantasy as high and low genres. Worse, the hegemony of realism also obliges careerist artists to do the propaganda work of neoliberalism: fettering our imaginations to the harsh reality that "there is no alternative."

The realist way of writing about and painting the world fits the scientism of the nineteenth century. If you depict what you see, you are making a claim about objective reality. What this overlooks is the reproduction of things the way they are, including the power relations that undergird the so-called fact. While realism shifted the focus of artistic representation to previously overlooked or marginalized characters, the texture of the reality they reproduced still knitted a tight web of limited possibility for their futures. The glimpse into the lives of misery led by rural peasants might have the benefit of leading a bourgeois lady to perform charity, but we could readily critique this material in the vein of voyeurism, relishing in the spectacle of suffering while shaking your head with that favorite liberal affect: moral outrage.

On the other hand, the second half of the nineteenth century also saw a move away from realism in the opening of what would later be called science fiction, supernatural stories, and above all utopian literature. The legacy of early European anarchist thinking coincides with the development of imaginative literature that serves to question the philosophical and political insistence that life must be this way. In Chapters 7 and 8, we see how anarchist ideas of time and space can help bring deviation from the so-called real as a way to disidentify from the power that holds us in its thrall and puts us back in touch with the power we have not ceded to the demands of the state.

Description as Prescription

The scheme of realist representation also served as a tool of colonial power. As Europeans invaded lands, slaughtered and enslaved the inhabitants, and extracted resources, they were also in the process of defining a concept of humanity through the not yet fully distinct fields of science and philosophy. Part of this process of normalization took place in the form of coherent narrative accounts (of encounters, of individual lives). Since Europeans judged people from within their own narrow definition, being able to fit these narrative standards helped define a sense of humanity. For example, the early slave narratives were often framed by abolitionists as proving the full humanity of the author (while they were also subjected to doubts that people who had been enslaved were capable of writing such accounts). The narrative moved from captivity to freedom, following a convention of humanization, in order to elicit "a sense of compassion for the miseries which the Slave Trade has entailed on my unfortunate countrymen," as Olaudah Equiano wrote in one of the first slave narratives in English. Along with conversion to Christianity, mastering the conventions of European literature was held to be proof that people of African descent—people turned into property and forcibly enslaved—deserved dignity. Of course, this approach doesn't end up destroying the dehumanizing premise—it fits within a reformist schema by meeting the oppressor on their terms, in their language. But this itself doesn't take away the power of these texts.

After (apparent) emancipation, this issue of representation morphed into the expectation for Black authors to be representatives of their race, and for their material to focus on a highly conventionalized "Black experience." In "Everybody's Protest Novel," James Baldwin argued against what he called "the protest novel," which he traced from *Uncle Tom's Cabin* to *Native Son*, as literature that might as well be a pamphlet, since it actually flattened "humanity" into issues. Therefore, even if there is a "good" political point to be made—like Stowe's novel playing a role in the historical retelling of the Civil War and emancipation—the ultimate effect is disastrous, since it confines Black experience to representations of degradation.

Realist modes of representation raise problems in matters of both space and time. As we will discuss, our practical anarchism wants to multiply or stretch our sense of time, to create the space for spontaneous event, and to refuse pictures of how life should be. In terms of narrative time, we see that each event, whether depicted as fate or chance, seems inevitable with a backward glance. If we tell stories to make sense of our lives and experiences, giving them a stable structure also makes it easy to feel like it couldn't be another way.

In terms of space, it is again a question of individual lives over many. Like the idea of an elected official representing a constituency, the limited focus of a novel swallows up the many lives that make things possible through webs of care within the depiction of the one. And just as the elected official supposedly standing in for the will of the people actually serves their own interest, or really the interest of the people who fund them, the protagonist stands in for the anonymous lives of everyone else. Not only do the lives of people who don't fit within the frame get left out completely, the protagonist is taken to be representative of a normal path, for the reader or viewer to identify with. This process of representation could also be looked at like the mass-produced piece of clothing (or any other consumer item). Within that shirt is a history of labor that can't be seen. The finished product pleases the eye but erases the lives and experiences of everyone along the way who had a hand in its production.

Ultimately, realism entails a politics of representation, limiting the choice of what fits into the world that gets represented. Ideology works as a lens to view the world, making some things comprehensible and others absent. The dominant ideology encodes certain things as possible and other things as fantastical. The aim of the practical anarchism proposed in this book is to remove the hegemonic lens to see the world outside the structures of domination. Novels that adhere to realist values of representation therefore end up replicating the existing power structure. But this happens even in non-capitalist art, like the Soviet-preferred socialist realism style. The Soviets silenced artists who experimented with form and content and failed to represent the world as the protectors of Leninist or Stalinist ideology saw fit. (And it made for boring art.)

On the other hand, if we think of anarchism as an ethical practice of liberation, rather than an ideology that can be applied or replicated (like socialist realism), then every choice in a novel or film or painting is imbued with liberatory—or oppressive—potential. When we come to read these works, or to watch the films or television programs, we come outside of simple identification with the characters or the dominant narrative, holding out for places of opposition tucked within the narratives themselves. We can form counterinterpretations of art, and in that perform an analysis of power systems. Often, what the Russian formalists called the "estrangement" of art can actually help us face the dominant meanings in a starker way, so that we can frame our alternate visions otherwise.

Art for Art's Sake, or Political Art?

Even when realism was establishing its dominance, there were already countercurrents to its hegemony. As we mentioned, Oscar Wilde, the famous British aesthete who was put on trial for "gross indecency" (a version of sodomy laws) and sentenced to two years hard labor for his sexual relationships with other men, flipped the understanding of Aristotelian mimesis in his epigram, "Life imitates Art far more than Art imitates Life." Though this may sound silly, Wilde's own life shows the seriousness of his claim. While on trial, he was forced to read from, and defend, the "improper" relationships between men in his novel *The Picture of Dorian Gray*. This novel also details the downfall of a celebrated aesthete, known for destroying the reputations of young men, so Wilde's own career was implicated in the plot of the novel. Not to simplify this relationship between Wilde's fate and Dorian's, we can see the underlying theoretical insight in Wilde's claim. We understand the world through the forms in which we perceive it, which includes artistic representation, and the art that we take in influences the ways we live. Think about how our ideas of love and romance are so saturated with unquestioned lines from boring songs and romantic comedies. Realism is a tautology, even with the most liberal aspirations to evoke sympathy for the plight of the ordinary person to a middle-class readership.

But Wilde's provocation, part of the Aesthetic and Decadent movements, caused a rift in the political understanding of art. Aestheticism promised an "art for art's sake," as a way to dismiss the moralism of bourgeois society. But this separation seemed to mean it took no political stance. This debate heightens in the aftermath of the Bolshevik takeover of the Russian Revolution, and then again after the struggles against fascism up to the mid-twentieth century. But the distinction between art for art's sake and politicized art created a false binary, seen to be a choice between aestheticism, which supposedly protected bourgeois values by isolating art from the world, and political art, which explicitly reflected political commitments. Like most binary choices, narrowing to two options leaves out room for complexity. Many people lumped into the art for art's sake category actually created deeply political work (especially since this attention to style was historically associated with what we might now call queer subcultures). On the other hand, overtly political art often misses the mark or ham-fistedly represent its own worldview. For example, modern conceptual art often tries to make a political point but ends up seeming self-absorbed, particularly as it often lives inside inaccessible galleries. Overall, we can see the Aesthetes and Decadents making a demand for beauty beyond survival; like the famous anarchist song, we want bread and roses too. Mimi Thi Nguyen insists in *The Promise of Beauty* that we look at how beauty keeps being claimed by the downtrodden even as it is often used as a tool of power.

Socially responsible art (which historically has focused on moral representation of life) often upholds a kind of realism as opposed to escapist fantasies. But as someone once said, "the usual enemies of escapism are jailers." Still, one can argue that realism is the most powerful political tool within the realm of art for upholding things the way they are. If we deem realism to be more serious than other forms of art because it represents the actual world (and ostensibly all the contradictions of it, serious "adult" problems like infidelity, etc.), this seems to demand from us that we accept the world the way it is. Scrupulous realism that tries to render mundane life in all its detail helps reproduce an ideology and a hierarchy of values. Maybe we do find a basic enjoyment in art that echoes our world back to us. But beyond that, we look to art to heighten our experience, to feel expansive possibility, to multiply our consciousness, to show that the awful world still holds some beauty.

Picture the World You Want

Our practical anarchist view of art then raises new questions. What if we don't represent the world with realism, reifying the way things are, but only represent the world in conflict against that or, even better, how we want it to be? More and more, it seems like the standard narrative in films and books has no reason to exist except to prop up the world as it is, to reify family structure, jobs, and life patterns: our position within the vast mechanism of the state. Every day we are inundated with narratives of inevitability. The long process of building up the state has made people more and more dependent on it, erasing stories of particularity with conventional expectations of how things must be. The seemingly innocent realm of realism turns from descriptive to prescriptive. We inherit structures of love and romance from marriage plots and pop songs.

Though the mainstream world might be caught up in fears of fake news, and might condemn art as escapist, we can see art instead as a place to begin practicing liberation now. There is freedom in reading— it has always been dangerous to authorities and parents—since when we read, no one else knows what is going on in our heads. Watching films, we can momentarily leave behind the boundaries of our world. We can exercise imagination to dissolve those bonds that keep us in identities, class positions, and jobs. Art is a space for us to begin our disidentification.

The state consolidates its power by a sleight of hand that art can forcefully oppose. Like détournement, we can think of other ways to use the same apparatus for our own ends. The state saps people's autonomy by substituting the things we do for ourselves with bureaucratic schemes that seem to promise ongoing solutions to problems but really just make us feel dependent on state infrastructure (and powerless to combat whatever arbitrary decisions come from the top down). We have immense fear of losing whatever services or claims we can make on the state, as if there aren't long histories of these things being done by communities themselves—and as if what the state gave us was actually enough. Watch how quickly we come to believe that things can't be otherwise.

The plots and temporality of stories transform endless possibilities into a singular outcome, through all the choices that are made. We know this in our own lives: we are told we could be anything, but when we look back, we see the path we ultimately took. Books like Le Guin's *The Dispossessed* and Piercy's *Woman on the Edge of Time* use a dialectical structure to transform our thinking from the closure of possibility to the opening of action. In both novels, the societies organized along anarchist ideas are set against other structures, whether the contemporary racial capitalist patriarchy or imagined versions of capitalism and state socialism. This doesn't serve merely as a comparative approach, where the reader decides, "I like this world better than the other." Instead, the multiplicity of worlds shows how an anarchist future is not a stable destination but the result of actions and analysis. State thinking holds us in the everlasting structures that seem inescapable, or that suture us into inevitability. In *Woman on the Edge of Time*, the character Connie's experience traveling to a genderless future of loosely connected anarchist communities brings her back to her contemporary moment of oppression in the 1970s, incarcerated in a mental institution, and from her experience she chooses a political act of revenge. The novel frames her unique personal act as inextricably linked with the opening of that beautiful future, even though she believes her life of abuse and neglect and state oppression is meaningless.

Art—whether we make it or enjoy it—can be a means to reject what we are given, to reject the false choices we are asked to make, and to begin to alter reality and reject the stranglehold of realism. We can even reject the art forms given to us to consume. The positive side of this would be the imagining of other possible worlds (even if it is shifting certain key details). In the aesthetic worlds we create, why would we need to have, for example, police acting the way they do in our world without active resistance? Why wouldn't there always be burning cop cars? Why would we represent the stifling aspects of the nuclear family as forever inescapable? Why have relationships stabilized in monogamous cis-heteronormative couplings? Why would we represent the inevitable progress of Western democracies into fascist rule rather than processes of liberation?

If our art is still beholden to representation—an undead relic of the nineteenth century—then we can use the "naturalizing" power of representative art to enact the different ways we want to live, whether that is in the way we represent queer/trans characters without major introductions, caveats, and explanations, or the way we show worlds without jails and police and government. But beyond this, the art we make and enjoy will negate what exists so we can escape.

Abstraction and "Difficult" Art

We can also look to abstract visual art, along with experimental music and contemporary poetry—art forms that get classified as bourgeois and/or inaccessible. In the heyday of abstract expressionism, many of the artists called themselves anarchists, for example Jackson Pollack and Mark Rothko. And yet the seemingly contentless art was seen by the CIA as an effective tool to combat potentially radical communist or socialist art, mostly expressed in forms of realism (Diego Rivera's murals, Richard Wright's novels), leading the CIA to find ways to fund and promote abstract expressionism. But I want to make a case for the liberatory potential of abstract or experimental art.

Perhaps a common experience is picking up a poem, or looking at an abstract painting, and feeling immediately shut down: "I don't get it." We are trained to look for deeper meaning in art, and when this meaning isn't apparent, when the typical cues of figural representation, or common syntax, are missing, we feel lost. This experience can make us feel stupid, or like the art is not made for us. In fact, this experience of exclusion has been used by the purveyors of highbrow art, whether gallerists trying to make money or academics trying to find a subject of study to cement their career, as a way to raise the stock in high art as a cultural value. However, as part of our practice of disidentification, we can refuse this exclusion and reorient our experience of art. When faced with art we don't immediately "get," we might then find different ways that we respond to it. A language poem without clear syntax might create strange associations and meanings; an abstract painting or noise music might produce heightened feelings and attention, if we open our ears and our eyes differently.

In the relief from needing to represent content or to replicate expected forms, these more "difficult" art forms put the prime space of interpretation in the momentary relationship that the viewer, reader, or listener has with the piece. We become the ultimate arbiter of the piece, and that might change moment to moment. In this moment, I find myself reactive to it—it's an experience (even a situation?), not a meaning. In this other moment, I reject its noise and the way it makes me feel. This kind of work takes away the authority of the artist, who offers the gestures that get frozen in space or time, and we can receive the gift in relation to however we feel at the moment. The roles of guest and host switch, we enter the house as guest and then become host, like Mrs. Dalloway, weaving a moment of coincidence and escape that ultimately lets us go.

We need to call on art to become the place of disidentifying. Not identifying with a hero or main character, not locking ourselves up in neat boxes of pride and oppression. Not identifying with the power structures and sources of dominance in family, gender, sexuality, race, and class. We want art that gives us a place to remove ourselves from identification with power, with the state, with conventions and plots. We want tastes and glimpses and foreshadowing of exercising our own power. We want art that opens us up to action—not to enlist us in a preordained future but to the indefinite and indescribable horizon of alternatives to the strangulating misery of what we are told must be. This comes from recognizing our own irreplaceability in self and community, so we can see that every act accumulates towards an unpredictable future, and that there is no essential separation between the powerful and powerless or between what is and what might be.

FAQs

Isn't art a waste of time?

Well, is wasting time so bad? That question comes from an overemphasis on productivity and work! Often politically minded people act like art is merely escapism, stealing attention away from real-world problems. While we have to insist that the pleasure of art is a necessity of life in its own right, we can also insist that art plays a role in our alternative world-building efforts. Furthermore, we might try to redefine what art is, taking it out of the high cultural protection of academics, critics, museums, and the market, to reposition it as certain kinds of activity and things we make to add pleasure and meaning to our life and our environment. In that definition, everyone is an artist, and life actually consists of artistic actions!

Can I watch guilty pleasures/trashy TV/Netflix?

While we might do well to be wary of the ways that corporate entertainment helps to fasten us into our scheduled lives of work and leisure, we also can't pretend that we can escape the impact of these cultural products on our lives. ("We live in a society," as the meme says.) Sometimes, I relate to these kinds of entertainment specifically like a drug—I seek it for a certain effect, usually a feeling of unplugging from work life and other demands. On the other hand, mainstream entertainment gives us a sense of the cultural atmosphere, and how much work goes into maintaining the status quo through representation. We can watch these things with a critical eye and for entertainment, to see how we are manipulated in every corner of our lives. We can enjoy ourselves while not identifying with the world this entertainment wants to preserve.

7

Who Will Fix the Roads and Collect the Trash? Anarchy in Your Neighborhood

- Giving up property relations
- Rethink the arrangement of our lives
- Anarchism happens in the spaces between us

Ceding Territory

One of the most famous anarchist slogans is Proudhon's "property is theft"—an often misunderstood claim. It points to the institution of private property, which became the foundation of the liberal nation state and capitalist economy through processes of settler colonialism and slavery. The condensed slogan turns on its head the concept of crime, pointing to the hierarchy of owners rather than the criminalization of the dispossessed. However, this idea tends to lead people to imagine that the idea of having any belongings is in some way oppressive. This misunderstanding has been turned into a joke: the meme about whether in full communism we all have to share a toothbrush. The answer that we can have our own toothbrush is instructive to navigating the areas between property as a formation of class and hierarchy (and even identity insofar as race is based on property, whiteness being defined through the rights to ownership of people and land), and the way we use the space and things in our world. An anarchist approach tends to think that our relationship to things and space has to do with use, not necessarily exclusive and eternal ownership based on contracts. Yes, I use my toothbrush and therefore it belongs to me. But would I be willing to relinquish it if need be? Our use of things doesn't preclude sharing or repurposing based on circumstances.

We can start to open up anarchist space as areas of overlap, of contiguity, in the mode of dual power or prefiguration. In this way, we can also begin to undo the borders that order our thinking and our world through imaginary partitioning into distinct parcels of land, property, objects, and beings. Everything is much more porous than that—we can simply think about how we live through our genders and sexualities, not ever reaching the idealized pole of the binary but in some relationship of failure to the seeming perfection. Similarly, no matter how much a country imposes border restrictions on its territory, it can never fully keep those borders "secure." Part of this fantasy is that any individual can be self-sufficient, taking nothing in from their surroundings (and producing no waste or by-product). When anarchists talk about autonomy, it's not the image of the sovereign citizen who owes no allegiance to anyone but themselves. It's a simultaneously individual and collective autonomy, a series of exchanges that gives us enough of a basis to live out our lives for ourselves, while also providing the necessary connections and collaborative care for us all to survive.

The fundamental relationship we ought then to have with our space is to rethink its usage as a process of opening that prioritizes collective liberation. How can we use space differently, so that we don't think of use as ownership but a form of sharing? There have been many different local movements to form community land trusts to try to turn the property structure imposed by the state over to people, to hold the land in common and use it against the individualized propertarian notions of ownership. If we think of ourselves as simultaneously guests and hosts, acknowledge that we have no innate belonging within any legitimate claim of rights and therefore remain open to the intrusion of others. Many non-Indigenous anarchists, following Indigenous thinkers, have a tendency to refer to Indigenous lifeways as an example of an alternative relationship to the land, one of "stewardship" not ownership, a relationship that does not impose strict and timeless definitions on use of space but that works in constant dialogue with the changes that happen in exchange of use and growth—another form of caretaking. But the non-Indigenous anarchist—the settler anarchist—must also reckon with being a settler on the land, another kind of guest, and cannot expect a free welcome to any kind of takeover. For settlers to rethink their relationship to space, we must reckon with our illegitimacy on the land and forge different relationships through different practices—not by expecting to be included in autonomous Indigenous spaces, but by undoing the settler logics that deem land as resource rather than relationship and knowledge.

As a settler on Turtle Island—land forcibly stolen by the so-called United States from Indigenous peoples who lived according to different relations compared to the propertarian basis of liberal republics—I try to rethink my occupation of space as temporary and not through ideas of ownership or even belonging. In the spirit of disidentification and dissolution, I want to inhabit these spaces—from the homes I make, to the cities, towns, and villages I pass through—so as to spread resources, share what there is, and make temporary homes for everyone. Houses can be used like the underground railroad in the nineteenth century, to shelter people on their way to freedom. We have to be ready to give up what we have when it is built with the blood of slavery and genocide. Even if you don't live on stolen land, you can embody this practice of doubling as guest and host, in order to free the land from this stranglehold and see it as a space that holds you in common with the others around you.

Colonialism, capitalism, multinationals, and states have created a situation in which people are surrounded by objects that are made with pieces that are extracted and imported from all around the world. It's the dystopian side of the liberatory idea of internationalism. Not international—or extra-national—solidarity but international consumption. Our entire cultures are made up of the products of globalized markets, where new "exotic" images and sounds are brought from the margins to the centers to pique the pockets of employed spenders. The supply lines are so invisibilized to us that we often don't realize that many of our staples of consumption are colonial products, with the obvious examples of coffee, sugar, and chocolate. And yet they bear no trace of these other places; consumer products are endlessly homogenous. We discussed the alienation of work, which turns our lives into waged hours to earn money for survival. But we can apply this idea to consumption too, such that the objects we use and consume, tied as they are to these bloody histories and current violent practices, seem to come to us ready-made from nowhere—another utopian dream.

Making Space Visible

If invisibilization is a major method of maintaining capitalist "realism," as Mark Fisher called it (making us believe in the inevitability and inescapability of capitalism), then perhaps a tactic when it comes to rethinking space is to make things visible: learning the history of the spaces we occupy, how they have come to be this way, who has lived here before, and what processes went on to remove some people and allow others to remain. There are concrete examples of things that are erased and made invisible: the prior histories of people living on the lands that have become the United States, Canada, Australia, New Zealand, and South Africa, to name just the Anglo settler colonies— an erasure that is ongoing. The prison system is another good example of invisibilization, and points to a shifting relationship to space in the current era of twinned capital and state forces. Prisons are mostly invisible in our landscape, except if you or your loved ones get ensnared in them or you live in a town where one has been built. The punishment system of restriction of movement—confinement or incarceration— came to replace exile along with the introduction of personal liberty and rights. Societies used to shun and exclude, now the state disappears you from social life, but not to another land. The seeming security of the city relies on the knowledge that there is a place—the prison— where all the bad people are locked up. But it's a space we never have to confront. However, according to ex-prisoner Farid Ben Rhadi, "[p]rison only exists to make those on the outside believe they are free."

Similarly, urban areas spilling over into slums is like a return of the repressed: the fact that you can't actually dispose of whole populations. This production of "surplus humanity" is part of the massive dispossession that Mike Davis writes about in *Planet of Slums*, where neighborhoods overflow and informal economies arise, alongside the booming prison population. Our systems produce waste and that waste doesn't actually disappear. In every city, we see the police and businesses wage war against unhoused people, trying to wish away the inequalities of property by evicting encampments. The infrastructural attempt to solve this problem is an item in urban geography—the projects of redevelopment. From the famous widening of the grandes avenues in Paris, in order to combat the possibility of the people barricading the streets against the police and military, to the removal of public housing in New York City to make the Lincoln Center and the Metropolitan Opera— or perhaps more obviously profit-driven, without the excuse of high culture, the way that New York's Times Square, as Samuel Delany analyzes in *Times Square Red, Times Square Blue,* was cleaned up of its porn theaters and sex shops, places for gay cross-class casual sex, under the excuse of public health (fearmongering around HIV/AIDS), security (crime against tourists), and family values, in order to create the Disneyfied chain store open-air mall that exists today.

Where do the people go? The economy needs its disposables, the "reserve army of unemployed," to keep wages low and profits high, and, echoing Ben Rahdi, to let a certain fraction of the population think it is really living. The state creates excluded populations, often described as undesirables, whether racialized, criminalized through citizenship or black markets, or turned into deviants through sexual norms. These populations can then be treated as an internal threat, added on to the external threat of other nations and migrants at the borders, so that the state can flex its security apparatus.

In these images of space, there is an idea of totalization and the desire to completely erase these undesirables—the genocidal urge that ultimately underpins state formation. In the Shoah perpetrated by the Nazis against the Jews, the Nazis attempted not only to eradicate the Jews but to erase the traces of having done so. Such attempts at erasure always prove to be an impossible task, as even the erasure leaves a mark. Similarly, the process of ideology naturalizes and invisibilizes the frameworks for how we inhabit the world, but it still leaves traces for us to track ourselves into new coordinates on the land. If we rethink our relationship to land and space along these lines, we can learn of tactics to resist domination and open spaces up for collective care. But first, we need to look at the way that the power systems structure the spaces we inhabit in Western urban/exurban spaces.

A World without Police

The very existence of the police is one of the main things that makes community and neighborhood (seem) impossible. And yet it is the police—whether visibly cruising more oppressed neighborhoods, or as a looming threat to settle disputes between middle-class white people—who maintain whatever cohesion there is to our current urban, suburban, and even rural geographies by force. Shifting away from the enforcement that keeps us living in these arrangements is a major element of disidentification that would allow people to find ways to connect around issues that actually affect their daily lives (as opposed to the alienated form of politics streaming in through our devices).

Kristian Williams details the history of the modern police force in the USA from an anarchist and abolitionist perspective in *Our Enemies in Blue: Police and Power in America*:

> In short ... the police exist to control troublesome populations, especially those that are likely to rebel. This task has little to do with crime, as most people think of it, and much to do with politics—especially the preservation of existing inequalities. To the degree that a social order works to the advantage of some and the disadvantage of others, its preservation will largely consist of protecting the interests of the first group from the demands of the second. And that, as we shall see, is what the police do.

The discourse around law and order, or crime and criminality, or even safety, gives an alibi to this actual violent enforcement arm of the state, by mystifying the relationship between the citizen and the police. As Williams writes, "the police represent the point of contact between the coercive apparatus of the state and the lives of its citizens."

But beyond the violent contact between a person and the police, we might extend the function of policing deeper into our institutions and even our own thinking and relation to others. The social order tries to frame all of our encounters through this logic. Mark Neocleous's *A Critical Theory of Police Power* is helpful because it pushes us to think beyond the literal police force to extend the policing function to the range of institutions that we have come to take for granted as state infrastructure. Tracing the history of these institutions, he shows that they originally developed out of police power. The police as an arm of the state that began to diversify into the various bureaucracies and services that keep us dependent on the goodwill of the state, while at the same time subjecting us to surveillance and violence in maintaining "order." Order comes not simply from disciplining our bodies into particular habits of movement, work, and consumption, but also through our investment in the institutions that come to fill out the state, or as Neocleous calls it, "administering civil society." In this definition, policing extends far beyond the actual implementation of laws; it is the power of the state to arrange our lives in all of its details, including such seemingly distant activities as clearing the roads of debris after a storm, or setting up neighborhoods along racial, class, and ethnic lines.

We can see this policing function internally as our expectation that "someone" (an authority) will handle any situation—it's not our problem. In fact, this would be part of the trade-off we get for relinquishing autonomy to the state, not having to deal with the mess. Not that the state deals with it any better, as we so often discover first hand. In the end, this relationship keeps us in a perpetual minority status, looking up to a powerful parent to fix things for us, rather than face our problems. Further, this trade-off comes at a higher expense than it might seem, since it constantly keeps us vulnerable to arbitrary state violence. The benign side of the administrative state cloaks the fact that at any moment the agents of the state, the actual police, can strike people down with impunity—and this goes for particular populations marked as more dispensable than others, such as racialized people, migrants or refugees, and unhoused people.

The existence of the police as physical agents of the state, whether or not they literally stand on the corners of your neighborhood, is necessarily linked to the policing function that we internalize, ranging from the internal cop that tells us not to shoplift, to our own inclination to inform on the actions of others, what the Ruth Wilson Gilmore describes as being on "guard duty." This inner cop is the prime site of our process of disidentifcation. From an anarchist perspective, this is an internalization of hierarchy, which abdicates responsibility for facing our own problems. The more that this type of policing becomes normalized, the further isolated we are from each other, stuck into family or household units, even if we live "non-traditionally," with no relationship to our neighbors or even the land we live upon.

Policing functions on this spectrum from guns and billy clubs and enforced racial, gender, and class violence, all the way to the centralized authority we call to intervene in any problem that seemingly affects us. When this is an inconvenience, say a problem with the roads, stray animals, or anything along those lines, we could just as easily call the police as the appropriate specialized agency (and we may not even question how these agencies end up linking together in the ultimate web of dispersed state power). When the problem comes to dealing with other people, it often connects to a fear of others created by the portrayal of "disordered" people as threats. This fear of others moves down to our avoidance of interpersonal conflict, our shying away from confrontation and disagreement.

"Civil society" as administered by police and politicians actually encompasses a massive range of violence. Just as capitalism and the state work to separate the realm of politics from the realm of economics, so that the economy seems neutral, they also work to remove society from the realm of politics, so that our involvement in politics comes through minimal symbolic gestures like voting rather than actually building our world, and instead we are handled by the various agencies of the state. Anarchists tend to be wary of the realm of official politics, since this realm works to replicate the status quo, and our involvement only acts as an endorsement. At the same time, we might politicize everything, or in other words remove the boundaries of the areas of our lives from being neatly ordered according to their logics. The state and the police lull us into inaction, deferring to authority, passing the buck, expecting outside help and intervention. We have deputized or professionalized problem solvers to abdicate us of responsibility of making choices, taking sides, resolving problems, and caring for each other. Our life flattens out. But then we must ask how anarchism might envision a rearrangement of our lives in the space we currently inhabit.

Will Anarchy Fix Capitalism's Ruins?

One objection that cynics make against anarchist visions of decentralized, loosely federated, autonomous, self-managed communities is the issue of infrastructure and the problem of scale. How can anarchists envision the enabling of big infrastructure projects like roads and bridges? A simple response is that just because it has fallen to the state (or the state propping up businesses) to do these projects doesn't mean this is the only or even best way to get things done. Take potholes for example. You can probably note in your neighborhood the limited repair that potholes get, especially depending on the area, how commercially driven it is, what the median house price is, etc. In 2017, anarchists in Portland, Oregon began filling potholes that had been ignored by city infrastructure. In response to liberal supporters of the state touting the need for centralized planning of infrastructure projects, they pointed out that the city's repairs never happen efficiently, if at all. In the spirit of direct action and mutual aid, the people of the community came together to fix a problem, thereby creating bonds with people living there who weren't involved in mutual aid or anarchist projects.

A more complex response to the infrastructure question would go into detail about how the state relates to public space and private property through periods of abandonment and then redevelopment for profit. Sure, big infrastructure projects were historically a means of employment used to aid some parts of the population—for example, during the Great Depression in the USA. But these projects only helped some people, usually falling along racial lines, and for the most part in the decades following the state abandoned these infrastructure projects.

This outcome is one of the ways neoliberalism shifted the way that the state manages its land, passing off more and more to privatized companies with no accountability (except to shareholders). Additionally, when people tout state infrastructure projects, they neglect to mention how many of these seemingly great projects decimate whole communities, for example, when a freeway breaks up a historically Black neighborhood in favor of commuter ease and tourist access. Every process of urban renewal and redevelopment has displaced poor and racialized people. Our roads plow through communities, solidify divisions of class and race, and frame our lives towards always working for more.

Therefore, an even more complex anarchist response would address how the infrastructure that builds the world we live in isn't made for our survival, not to mention sustainability of life on the planet. The infrastructure questions must contend with the possibility that the things that need fixing are only symptoms of the larger, unmanageable, broken world we live in. For example, the post-World War II development of the United States centered around families: households as individual and atomized units of consumption, producing a layout of highways leading from suburbs to cities, with individual workers driving alone in their cars from home to job. The interstate system replaced the railroad, which was already a driving force of colonization and genocide, and it became easier and cheaper to drive alone rather than to take collective forms of transportation. In Europe, similar developments occurred in terms of creating work lives based on commuting, though the infrastructure of the state and the closeness of geography allowed access to railways (previously put in place as part of the movement of goods made from colonial spoils and the shipment of coal to power industry).

Life has become arranged such that everything is done elsewhere. You work in one place, live in another. Children grow up and move away to make a life (i.e. get a job). Food is shipped in from elsewhere. The products you consume are made who knows where. This process is indicative of the centralization of the state and the market as a whole, where individuals and communities are made dependent on these supply lines for survival. We fall into a statist state of mind when we think of the infrastructure we have inherited as a good in itself, rather than trying to rethink ways to organize our world, time, resources, and relationships to provide what we need.

It is here that the problem of scale comes in, seemingly to reattach us to the state as the only solution to (its own) problems. Put simply, the problems we face are so large, it's hard to imagine local solutions to them. This reaction does abdicate some agency, however, to alter conditions where we stand. A good example of this thinking relates to the ongoing climate catastrophe. Even leftists have a hard time imagining a solution to this other than a globalized federation of states addressing the problem. However, we might also see that the state itself is dependent on the extraction and destruction that is causing climate catastrophe. How can we use the same instrument for resolution? Certainly, the answer favored by state and capitalist forces—individualized solutions of consumer choices such as decreased consumption—aren't a solution in themselves either. But even the more progressive ideas of encouraging the self-limitation of corporations, or punishing infractions against limits, don't go far enough to halt an irreversible situation that instead calls for adaptation. From our perspective, we can refuse to participate to a certain extent, but that in itself won't destroy global supply chains, agricultural industry, or military expenditure, and all of the damaging resources used to fuel them.

The global Covid-19 pandemic is a good example of this contradiction. Many people witnessed local organizations pool resources, time, and risk exposure to help make sure that their neighbors had what they needed. In my area, mutual aid groups formed out of previous catastrophes—in response to hurricane seasons that decimated multiple communities. In fact, we already had the infrastructure and networks in place to put together hotlines, make deliveries, gather resources, and eventually find a place to locate a free store. So in a way, this gives the lie to the infrastructure question. As Eric Laursen points out in *The Operating System: An Anarchist Theory of the Modern State*, most of the social services that we've come to expect from the state were first started as mutual aid projects that then got co-opted by the state, thus diluting their revolutionary beginnings and eventually stripping them away. This experience happens again and again whenever disaster comes up.

As communities, we simultaneously need to defend ourselves against the state's violence and against the disasters brought on by the state and the market.

When crisis hits, people do what needs to be done—no matter that the media narratives are about crime and danger. In the end, the state often co-opts or takes credit for whatever element of mutual aid doesn't threaten its ultimate legitimacy. What doesn't fit gets labeled "crime," and becomes an excuse for ramping up security measures. For example, scott crow describes in *Black Flags and Windmills: Hope, Anarchy, and the Common Ground Collective* how, during the aftermath of Hurricane Katrina in New Orleans, there was media hype on looting and violence, but the reality was that groups on the ground took care of one another and the violence they faced was from white supremacists and the police. The confusion is caused by the fact that these kinds of crises level the typical property barriers while also amplifying the need for basic sustenance, so that people end up "looting," which is just reappropriating their necessities for survival (and sometimes even luxury items, as we discussed in Chapter 5).

There is a myth about organizing—that problems can only be solved once sufficient organizing has happened. It's the same myth as infrastructure and scale. These myths claim that novel solutions are needed for ongoing problems, that we aren't doing enough, when the truth is that we are already doing the work. In the same way that the emphasis on waged labor obscures all the other forms of labor that we do just to maintain our existence, the logic of institutions obscures the organizing and infrastructural work we do in informal and communal ways to make our lives livable within this difficult context. Now, just as wanting to orient our lives against work requires us to acknowledge that work extends beyond the job to all the other labor we do in our lives, we have to acknowledge what we have already done to make our lives livable despite the state maintaining its social war against us.

But we also have to remember and be open to the fact that, outside of work, outside of the state, things will look different. We don't want big organizations of bureaucrats making decisions, just like we don't want armed professionals with the dispensation to use violence resolving our conflicts (police). We don't want to work for bosses, but we can direct our energy and efforts to life-making and world-building willingly.

Shifting Our Social Space

Let's return to the idea from *Wages against Housework*, which suggests that naming the unpaid work we do as work enables us to imagine a world without work: one in which we might truly live and learn what love is. A radical take on "social reproduction" would have to think about how to reproduce conditions of living that transform relationships of exploitation. In the situation of infrastructure and administration, professionalizing services that enable people to work at their jobs means relieving them of the tasks of maintaining the world around them. In fact, it is a furthering of our alienation from the world, since all of these frames end up making it so that we can't see outside of them: home, work, market, restaurant, café, school, bar. The public spaces are emptied of life and only orderly use is permitted: a playground, a dog run, places for exercise. Our lives are compartmentalized such that we feel we need outside agencies to maintain its borders.

The fact is that we really do most of the work that helps us maintain our lives, even at this low level of existing. We take out our own trash. We find ways to feed ourselves, clothe ourselves, and perhaps clean our clothes, our bodies, and our homes. Rather than relieving ourselves of the work it takes to keep our lives running, we can refocus our lives around what actually goes into living them—what would truly serve us. I go back to Colin Ward's description of home handiwork and the use of tools in *Anarchy in Action*. The consumer market created a range of more accessible power tools that enable people to create and undertake projects on their own as amateurs. However, the tools themselves are still expensive, and the common experience is having to buy a tool for single or only occasional use. The solution Ward envisions is "pooling of equipment in a neighbourhood group," resulting in a community workshop. This example concentrates almost all of the aspects of life we have been describing. Ward uses this idea to get into the organization of work (and its relationship to leisure). But here also

we see the issue of property: the isolation of our lives into tiny economic units pretending to be self-sufficient. And then a solution that
literalizes the world-building through actual tools in a shared network.
If our neighborhoods were organized along these lines, with spaces
of shared resources, from tools to childcare to communal meals, we
could imagine a complete shifting of the time and space of our lives that
would allow us to face our problems with a different sense of energy,
support, and possibility.

In this reframing, then, I hope to turn back the question of infrastructure. To reshape our world outside, beyond, and against the state and
the market, we would have to question radically the way our lives are
plotted and arranged. The very geography of our world is the outcrop-
ping of colonialism, racial capitalism, and the borders of nation states.
Our cities were built to enable the concentration of wealth through
the exploitation of labor. They've been further arranged to segregate
communities, cut off the possibility of rebellion, and divide starkly all
the commonly shared space into private property and publicly policed
zones. On top of it all, if you live in a country like the United States,
the settler state is in a continual process of erasure and genocide of the
Indigenous people who have been displaced to form this land.

Even living in a city, in the midst of gentrification, we see the redevelopment of services towards a tourist industry rather than serving the
needs of a "community." In the city I live near, there is no central grocery
store and no cheap market—only boutiques, art galleries, breweries,
crystal shops, and high-end vintage stores. Likewise, there is no convenient public transportation. The city isn't arranged to make life easy for
the people living there but rather to make an imaginary space for tourists to consume the "flavor" of that city. The majority of property gets
bought up by absentee landlords who rent out Airbnbs, which makes
it nearly impossible to afford housing. People live further and further
away from the places they are forced to work, making us more reliant
on our own transportation vehicles and gasoline. I have piled up these
examples in order to push towards reframing our questions around
what we actually make use of to better our lives.

In the conclusion of her monumental overview of rioting and looting in the USA, Vicky Osterweil writes beautifully about the alienation of these urban spaces and the repurposing of them through collective action:

> A CVS Store in Baltimore, a Brooklyn Duane Reade, a St. Louis QuikTrip: these are not meant to be historical places. In fact, an entire science, incorporating marketing, psychology, architecture, and interior design is devoted to giving corporate spaces like these a sense of the timeless infinite present of consumption and stripping them of the possibility of change, of difference, of politics, of history. But struggle can turn even the most consciously constructed banality into a place of rupture, community, transformation, and liberation.

All of these locations became space for action and care within the context of uprising. This is another instance of repurposing the resources that surround us towards our own ends. It isn't the solution to all of the problems that we face, but we can use the remains of the infrastructure for temporary collective support. Shifting our perspective, disidentifying from the power structures that create this "world of banality," we can see instead the materials of our liberation. As infrastructure crumbles and the state abandons us, these remnants no longer serve their apparent purpose, and so we can create worlds within them. My argument here, then, is to rethink our social spaces, our neighborhoods, through the lens of uprising, of riot, but with a view towards making them ultimately livable. In those moments of eruption, people living near one another tend to collaborate against a common threat of the state rather than remain siloed in the individual units of house and family. Can we inject this momentary feeling into our daily lives outside of insurrection?

Community Self-defense as Care Work

Anarchists tend to think of community self-defense in response to the various threats posed by the state and its unofficial representatives, like white supremacist vigilante groups. This tradition, like many, goes back to the Black liberation struggles, where Black people armed themselves against the terror and violence routinely visited upon them by police, the KKK, and just run-of-the-mill racists. In communities that are prone to institutional violence, there is also a need to take conflicts within the community into their own hands, without relying on the intervention of the state services that many white middle-class people will call upon to solve their problems.

This tradition of community self-defense often gets called violence by the state, particularly when it comes to armed Black militants protecting themselves against white vigilante violence. In the face of threat, community enclaves organize in the moment to protect themselves. The untold side of the "civil rights" or Black freedom movement of the 1950s and 1960s is the story of this kind of protection, especially since the existence of Black freedom fighters was an immediate threat to the state. In a different context, we see this kind of mobilization today on a larger scale in countering fascist demonstrations globally. A lesson of antifascism is deplatforming, kicking them off the streets, trying to stop any hold they can get. This type of confrontation goes back to the beginnings of fascism, but it has persisted in subcultural spaces when fascism creeps in, and now in a larger global fascist rise it results in street movements.

But the other side of this kind of self-defense against the state, and its deputized agents like fascists, is a kind of care work. Care and self-defense go hand in hand. They make each other possible. I mean this both literally, in the sense that care is necessary to enable the work of self-defense, and more expansively, in the vision that care and self-defense are two major ingredients for reshaping our immediate world as a place we can live. In my view, we ought to prioritize these care networks themselves as self-defense. As we build and change our relationships through clear communication, understanding of boundaries, and aiming our connections towards mutual autonomy and the ability to ask for help, we create the initial steps of reframing "infrastructure" through the actual needs we experience.

Marronage, Displacement, Abandonment

The capture of space through the totalizing aims of the state and capital actually produces waste spaces, appendices, abandonment, slums, and other spaces for potential reorganization. We can move from the contradictory space of care under discipline through our anarchist repurposing of space to the precedent of marronage. Russell Maroon Shoatz, a Black anarchist prisoner, has catalogued the North American history of maroon communities, consisting of fugitive slaves, Indigenous people, and white people living together in spaces outside the settler, plantation control, trading with neighboring communities, conducting raids, and welcoming further exiles. It's a different liberation of space than the dropout, back to the land communes of the hippies, which usually resulted in some patriarchal white (abusive) situation. Maroons lived on outskirts but in resistance to the dominant culture. They weren't strict enclaves but organic communities, with porous boundaries for entry and exit. And as Shoatz describes, these were the "real" and mostly "hidden" resistance to slavery, overlooked for more spectacular (and failed) rebellions. It is the hiddenness, perhaps, that allowed for success and longevity. Political occupations of space, like the movement of the squares and Occupy Wall Street, were set up in explicit and direct confrontation, marking out their resistance and often calling down the most extreme repression of state forces. Occupations can be effective in ending certain developments or even toppling governments, but they don't exist in the same fashion as maroons, which carve out lateral space within, beyond, and against the regime. They are in a state of siege, but their longevity allows for the world-building and care that goes into reproducing free space.

Perhaps the urban spillover of slums is actually proof of the exorbitant life that cannot be contained. There is a common anarchist propaganda graphic of plants reclaiming the world from buildings, police, and the state: through the cracks of the sidewalks, we see the grass always squeezing through. Green anarchists talk about rewilding, ways to undo the domestication of the planet and its life-forms (of course, like many other terms this has been co-opted to be largely emptied of its meaning). The relationship this entails means not prioritizing human life over plants and animals (sometimes referred to as more than human), but finding a way to create ecosystems that are not based on destruction: an attempt at mutual thriving. Some versions of this on a small scale may be seen in permaculture, where agriculture is done through an understanding of specific needs of the climate and land and research into ways to organize the use of land through planting in ways that promote biodiversity and long-term use. Still, permaculture by settlers does not address the fact of stolen land—this kind of project in itself isn't liberatory without further social connections.

European thought has placed the human at the center of all systems, as if everything has been organized, planned, and created to aid the production of this species. At the very least, a decentering of this anthropocentrism can produce a different way of thinking about space. Anarchism is a process of this displacement. One use of the term revolution was applied to Copernicus's "discovery" that the earth rotates around the sun—a heliocentric worldview. In *The Accursed Share*, the French thinker George Bataille uses the sun to reframe our place in the world and our thinking of economy through the gift: "The origin and the essence of our wealth are given in the radiation of the sun, which dispenses energy—wealth—without any return. The sun gives without ever receiving." In the vision of the world that Bataille generates through grounding it in the incessant pouring of sun energy, humans are just another excrescence, an outgrowth of this endless spending of energy that crystalized into a certain form of life.

The anarchist text *Desert* tries to look frankly at the condition of the climate crisis and the failure of revolutions to propose a different way of imagining liberating spaces while the world organized by state and capital continues more or less on its deathly trajectory. The anonymous author of *Desert* gives up on the idea of revolution as a possibility, especially in terms of the romantic notion of a massive anarchist revolution in which entire populations are convinced of the merits of anarchism. The place of intervention, they suggest, is in the interstices, the margins: "even if an area is seemingly fully under the control of authority there are always places to go, to live in, to love in and to resist from. And we can extend those spaces." We desert revolution, but we reclaim the deserts of capitalism, state, and climate catastrophe. Shifting away from the global perspective to local intervention, opening and defending liberated spaces to practice anarchism—in all its forms of autonomy, sharing, living within not on the land, organizing, or rising up. The practice of anarchism, they remind us, citing Colin Ward, is in fact the most convincing way for people to see its benefits. Anarchism is not simply a critique that promises a new world at some unknown point but a way that we build the world. Though hierarchy, dispossession, and domination—maps, states, roads, cities—seem to cover all of the land, anarchism creeps up and peeks through.

FAQs

Don't we need a state to take care of all the basic aspects of our lives?

The long project of the state and capitalism has been to make people dependent on their institutions for basic necessities instead of determining their lives for themselves. So in a way, the shape of our lives "needs" the state—but we don't get to determine that shape or prioritize other needs. In other words, the state causes the problem and then purports to fix it—while always decreasing the actual resources it gives us. We should take all we can from the state, no question; but we must also imagine ways of living that don't depend on an external centralized authority imposing its structure on us to keep us orderly and complacent. In moments when the state clearly fails—like climate disasters—people spontaneously organize to provide support. This principle is anarchy in action, as Colin Ward put it.

Can I have my own toothbrush?

Of course! There is the false assumption that sharing resources in common means that no one can have anything for themselves. But this is a misunderstanding of property relations. The kind of property we want to destroy is that upheld by violence through the police and the state: property that allows some to accumulate to the detriment of the many, property that destroys the world and our relationship to eco-systems. Having a toothbrush that you use—a tool that bears some intimacy—does not deprive anyone else of the possibility of brushing their teeth. Likewise, we can imagine a world in which we have space for solitude. Communal living doesn't have to mean everyone processing everything together with no space. We don't want the borders of nation and state, but we do want boundaries between our selves and others—only then can we form relationships, share our resources, and make sure we have what we need.

8

When Will It End?
Anarchy, Time, and the World

- Let go of progress narratives and one-time revolution
- Everything must end
- Anarchism is practice

Love Comes in Spurts

Our lives under capitalism are driven by clock time, hours of productivity, myths of work–life balance, and labor vs. leisure. As we get more integrated into online networks and labor can be remote or virtualized, the on and off of the clock seems to fade away. The so-called freedom of the gig economy to determine when you work becomes, due to low pay, an endless availability for labor. Similarly, "revolutionary time" can be another force of domination, as our commitment to revolution is measured by how fully we stake the totality of our lives for the cause. The problem is, this revolutionary time is always "to come," and too often enshrines a masculinist vision of the important work to be done, thereby neglecting the daily moments of care where we actually sketch out our freedom with each other, in relationships.

Here again, we take our lesson from feminist thinkers. Saidiya Hartman, writing from within and speculating about the experience of Black women at the turn of the twentieth century in the USA, puts forth the "wild idea" that "a revolution in a minor key" can be discovered and imagined in the lives of "young black women as social visionaries and innovators," "radical thinkers who tirelessly imagined other ways to live and never failed to consider how the world might be otherwise." The stories of such minor revolutions don't get told, since they occur within an unrecognized time and place, but in some ways, that's also precisely the power of potential escape. In the lives of young Black women she glimpses from between the archives, Hartman shows us "amplified moments of withholding, escape and possibility, moments when the vision and dreams of the wayward seemed possible." And she locates, in these moments, the bigger possibility: "At any moment, the promise of insurrection, the miracle of upheaval: small groups, people *by they-selves*, and strangers threaten to become an ensemble, to incite *treason en masse*." Living our lives in "everyday anarchy" frees us to our own desires, but also opens us up to unexpected connections—precisely the kinds that might burst out into rebellion.

To return to the context of classical anarchism, we can understand time through the concept of "direct action" or "propaganda by the deed." Both of these ideas, which are intimately connected, imagine a breaking into the imposed social order of hierarchy of a different time and space, the irruption of anarchism in the midst of normal life. When we manage our own lives, take action for the ends we want, or enact anarchism through our very lives, we alter the conditions of time and space that the state and capital order us within: outside of linear time and notions of progress and development. We also return, then, to the spontaneous order that we as living creatures create collectively.

Similarly, anyone who has participated in street movements or actions—especially a riot—knows intimately the shifting of time and space that can occur. These moments are in direct confrontation with the social order but unfurl a new order of collectivity, where people work together to open space and time for joyous destruction, commu-nal luxury, and an immediate feeling of life and of what life could be if we are free. Anarchists try to get us to think of these moments of upris-ing, rebellion, and riot, not in terms of a great wave that will build and finally turn the tide of revolution into a before and after, but instead a great reservoir of experience; events that we always live in relation to—untimely echoes across history of the memory of freedom that tell us there is always resistance to the dominant order, that life always exists otherwise, even, or especially, when you can't see it.

The experience of being on the streets with comrades creates a new sense of connection and bond, a new trust that can develop into lifetime relationships of collective care. But in this chapter, I want to propose ways we can reorient ourselves to time so that these moments don't only come in the exceptional and spontaneous uprising: we can dis-identify with the dominant order of productive linear time and progress and shift the emphasis onto our daily lives, allowing the time of our lives to loosen from the grip of linearity. In the in-between moments, can we find the same kind of care and collectivity that strengthens us in our liberation as we experience in direct confrontation?

The Disabled Time of Refusal

The disability justice movement tries to rethink the idea of capacity outside of the demand for productivity, in order to establish limits and boundaries on how much is asked of us and how much we expect our selves to give. "Spoon theory" helps us think of our actual capacity through the figure of a limited number of spoons, with each task—no matter how minute—taking up one spoon. Visualizing our capacity in this way allows us to know when we lack capacity and therefore orients us towards time differently. Disability is often treated as a liability, with unpredictable needs that disrupt productivity. But disabled wisdom in fact has a more realistic understanding of what goes into our survival. From the perspective of disabled people, we can more explicitly acknowledge the way we rely on the care of others to live. People cooking meals for each other, doing errands, helping find transportation, covering for each other when capacity is low, being able to process the difficulties of expectations, limits, and chronic pain. All of these things are demands on our time that seem to take us away from the forward momentum of production and progress. And yet they are the necessities of life— or better, they are living. We are continually asked to take our attention away from the ways we actually live, in order to put all of our effort into surviving according to the system's own needs. Disabled time is a refusal to clock in that allows for the expansion of these moments of mutual care that actually contribute to our living on in the world.

In *Care Work*, Leah Lakshmi Piepzna-Samarasinha propose a "fair trade emotional labor economy" that centers the experience of queer/disabled femmes of color, since people fitting these categories are typically put in the place of being expected to do necessary things for free. She describes the organizing of care as a "superpower" of sick and disabled people, navigating a world that is not only actively built towards our failure but intrudes on our autonomy. One basic feature of her proposal, based on reflecting on the ways she had been asked to do care work by femmes or people of color as opposed to cis men, is that the requests for help relate to the person as one who might not currently be able to provide that labor (consent), and also the kind of work that is reciprocal and deserving of gratitude. They are gifts, but not to be taken for granted. Creating the network of care means that you too may be asked to offer care.

The most important part of Piepzna-Samarasinha's proposal from our point of view is that it highlights refusal. Saying no is the refrain of this book. But I want to go beyond thinking of resisting or refusal as merely reactionary to the world as it is. It's not simply saying, "I don't want to." The refusal might operate more along the lines of Herman Melville's famously inscrutable legal clerk, Bartleby. When his boss (the narrator of Melville's story) asks him to do any task, he responds, "I would prefer not to." There is a subtlety in this refusal that opens a timeline for another world, one that perhaps coexists with the one trying to plug Bartleby into work. Of course, Bartleby ends up dying in prison, which would be one place the state can locate threats to their temporal order. He is forced to correspond to his limitations, rather than to escape with the split infinitive that never names the verb of his refusal. Before the punctual end, he works in the dead letter office, and here we can imagine again a suspension, a holding back from the onward motion demanded of us, a refusal just shy of confrontation that allows us to circulate undetected, undelivered.

Stretching Time to Incapacity

If you trace care back to the situation of infants, who literally cannot take care of themselves, it shows that care is a relationship, not a quantum of work. And if you have been a caregiver in any situation, you might know that care stretches time. It's not easily quantifiable in hours. Similarly, the experience of needing care—of being ill, for example—is one that disrupts the orderly sense of time, not to mention the demands of a linear productivity. For those of us caught up in the endless drive of work life, these experiences, especially if you are a caregiver, can feel like they are pulling us out of our duty—to work. And yet that work doesn't actually allow us to survive. For those of us who are chronically ill, we also have the experience of endless time: an unmarked time of repetition, illness, recovery, exhaustion, insomnia, anxiety.

As a caregiver for a child, I find myself constantly fighting against the expansive time and space of childhood so that I can return to my "work" despite my own hatred of work. As if the other world that I am supposedly fighting for is the work world, not the child's world. To watch my mind pit serious labor against the irresistible world of childhood—the imaginary, the nonsensical, endless conversations, exploring, walking around and around the house constantly in experiments—shows me to what extent I have internalized this drive forward. (Caring for a child has also made me face my own authoritarian proclivities.) As a chronically ill person, I also know that my productive time can always and unexpectedly be cut short—and in those times, I will rely upon the care of others, who will similarly feel the contradictory tug of their work and their love.

From all of this reflection, I propose an alteration of time towards a thought of (in)capacity. What do you want to do? Can you do it? Do you have time and space for it? To put it beyond the individual: does this collective arrangement work? If not, move on to something else that works. Some of this is easier said than done, especially since we have responsibilities to others through our relationships of care. But it may help us reflect on those relationships to think about whether they actually do what we want or need them to do. In this way we move from the ethics of duty—of owing that can quickly get collapsed into an economic sense—towards the ethics of the gift that Mauss describes: a fundamentally time-altering situation that creates obligation in the form of relationship. When I give the gift of my time and capacity it opens a new, discontinuous timeline, which only returns unpredictably from the other people I have formed bonds with. I may expect it, but I can't pin it down. It's the return of a delay, like the sound effect that repeats the end of the strum of a guitar at intervals. We can all get to things in our own time, outside the constant crush of crisis and the millions of overlapping timelines where worlds meet in miraculous connection.

This perspective then resituates our relationship to the world through our desires, which create their own timelines. I am writing from a perspective of queer liberatory time here, to reframe the world and time through desire—not the desire to produce or consume but the desire that has no single object. Think about falling in love: the world stops, and endless time produces that wonder of mutual discovery. Think about sex: the infinite time of caresses, smells, breathing—especially outside the domination of the orgasm, minutes and hours are indistinguishable. Desires open up possibilities without filling them in.

These open moments are the anarchy of our lives that we already live. They are the moments before the door closes: in-between day and night, the insomnia of endless time, where an hour feels eternal, and yet the clock keeps ticking towards the inevitable demand to wake and work. Thus, the endless nonlinear time of anarchism knows intimately the time of trauma, another kind of timelessness, another repetition and return, where intergenerational experiences of violence and resistance find their way into our present, a textured present, like geological layers, the fossil record of death and brutality, but also a testament to persistence and existence, untimely healing.

We can connect this thought of time and history to a relationship to our ancestors: people whom we choose to inherit and welcome into the present. The anarchist model of time would also connect to that invitation, of hosting guests from out of time, so that the bubbling up of other ways cannot be forgotten. Even in our supposed individuality, we are not alone but always haunted by all the modes of being and histories that we may not even consciously know. This goes just as well for our own experiences, which layer upon each other to form whatever we are in the moment. We can actively shape our situations, but we are equally shaped by them.

We can zoom out to geological time to see that human forms of social organization have their own boundaries, just as species and environments change and shift. An ecological perspective would shift the focus from human dominance and extraction of the earth's resources towards a different timescale, not based on continual progress that actually covers over histories of trauma and violence, but a flexible relationship to the natural surroundings that tries things out and gives up what causes harm. In the face of impending climate disaster caused by capitalism and the nation state, we have to acknowledge the fact that humans as a species are also a finite phenomenon—we came about and will eventually disappear. Thus, like we invite others into our space and time, we have to understand ourselves as guests—perhaps unwelcome ones. As settlers, for example, on Turtle Island, we continue to occupy land that was not willingly given. We have no right or claim to domination or use of this world, and we exist in tandem with all the other forms of life, more than human creatures, landscapes, and ecosystems.

Anarchist time allows for glimpses of these other systems to intrude upon the world, and it is from this concurrence of time and space that we begin to carve out our freedom, something that we must already have in some (in)capacity, in order to be able to open it up to an unknown future.

No Future?

As I've been suggesting, anarchism helps us think how to end things. Not simply ending the rule of the state and racial capital over our lives, but also dissolving situations, relationships, and institutions that no longer help us live our lives. In Ursula K. Le Guin's novel, *The Dispossessed*—which features an anarchist colony on the moon, Anarres—as the settlers organize their infrastructure around a central city, Abbenay, they have to keep in mind "that unavoidable centralization was a lasting threat, to be countered by lasting vigilance." In large part, the novel depicts the failure of this vigilance, how infrastructure ossified in such a way as to let power inhere in a single place. The main character, Shevek, has to become an anarchist among "anarchists" in order to counter the tendency of the Anarresti to rely on social pressure and informal power to maintain the status quo, as well as to end the anarchist colony's attempt to isolate itself from its seeding world, Urras. Anarres's removal makes sense to the extent that non-capitalist/non-state societies tend to face aggression from other states. The people of Anarres fear that the capitalist or state communist nations on Urras may still try to wipe out the anarchist colony, even decades after its founding. But Shevek also learns that anarchism must be continually tested by difference or it will solidify into informal power structures.

Shevek leaves Anarres against the wishes of the "empowered" councils of Anarres, in order to share scientific information that will ultimately lead to a new technology of instantaneous communication. I am using this paraphrase to set up my arguments about anarchist space and time. In the closing off of Anarres, the anarchist utopia, from communication with other worlds, we find also the desire to freeze time, to maintain the founding moment of anarchism and therefore block change. The desire to stop time and change is often the failure of utopian visions, since it relies on a dead world and is ultimately what produces the hypocrisy of the anarchist society in the novel. This is why the invention of instantaneous communication poses a threat to the world order, whether "anarchist" or authoritarian, since it allows ideas to seed in an unpredictable way—it maintains the future as an unknown, not a reproduction of the present.

But an actual practical anarchism opens itself to contingency. From Proudhon on, anarchism has embraced spontaneity—and anarchists have shown how there is informal and temporary order in spontaneity. The emphasis on contingency, discord, and dissolution is one of the main distinguishing factors anarchism has in relation to certain versions of Marxism, which try to elaborate a science of history and thus of revolution, envisioning stages of evolution from capitalism to communism. In a similar vein, liberals and party leftists get frustrated with anarchistic organizing when the formations refuse to make demands or don't normalize themselves into party structures and stand for elections. The liberal logic goes that some form of organized resistance must make a demand to power in order to be legible to the power structure—which can then decide on a concession to end the conflict. A leftist critique will evince a similar logic of legibility, though with less emphasis on the aim of reform (but to the same effect). Both agree that a formal and lasting structure must form in order for the state to recognize the counterpower. This problem of no demands or structure was widely reported on during Occupy Wall Street, where news media continually dismissed the occupation as not serious because it did not issue a political or party platform. The lack of demand, however, produces the possibility of an anarchist time. Anarchists don't make demands because our demands are impossible. The demand is to end the world as it stands. And power will never concede to that.

Starting from Erica Meiner's claim that "liberation under oppression is unthinkable by design," the abolitionist Mariame Kaba pushes us, in *We Do This 'Til We Free Us*, "to imagine and organize beyond the constraints of the normal," such that "imagining liberation under oppression" becomes "completely thinkable." For Kaba, this is an approach to the "everyday," the "mundane." Similarly, Dean Spade, Morgan Bassichis, and Alexander Lee suggest, in "Building an Abolitionist Trans and Queer Movement with Everything We've Got," that "impossibility may very well be our only possibility." In fact, they say, for queer and trans people, our life is a form of impossibility, a surplus to the cisheterosexual social order that regulates the reproduction of capitalism and the state. In the wake of all these abolitionist perspectives on impossibility, I want to push us to orient ourselves to the everyday, the in-between moments of time, as a space in which we can experiment, play, and reframe our lives through anarchism.

The word revolution, which has come to mean a disruptive change in an order, also contains the meaning of a return. This image could be seen in the repeated power changes in unstable regimes. But the current idea of revolution we use relies on a linear view of history, which as Hannah Arendt points out in *On Revolution* develops from the Christian timeline of the unique event of the coming of Christ. This coming is the beginning point of history—and revolution would be an endpoint (modeled on the apocalyptic Revelation), like the famous end of history claimed by the capitalist nations after the fall of the Berlin Wall.

But if revolution posits a total change of order, a new world, we might ask how we ensure that the new world is good and lasting.

The anarchist response is we don't and we can't! Shevek's experience on Anarres shows us that a liberated social order isn't a single event (ending time as we know it) but one that demands "lasting vigilance," something I revise as "perpetual care," a different orientation of care, framed through trans and disabled experience and marked by refusal, boundaries, and collective processes. As we have been putting these ideas together, we start to build a different way of relating to every aspect of our daily lives. Conflict resolution with a transformative approach looks at the messiness of our relationships and allows us to try and fail and try again. Transforming the way we relate to each other—and the world in which we do it—will take a ton of work: not the kind of labor that is extracted from us under capitalism but a kind that engages us in the world. This work is not punctual, nor does it have a timetable. Lasting vigilance is in fact a time of care for the world, failure and recovery is the time of engagement, the mess is the time of our lives unspooling around us outside narrative confines.

Time Out of Joint

The ideas of anarchism I present here as a practical engagement with the world do not form a map that promises our arrival in a new world. We can't form a vanguard party that will lead the masses to the promised land. Instead, these ideas of anarchism claim that some of what we have is already there, wherever it is, or on the way towards collective liberation. We need to attend to the current moments of anarchy in our daily lives. If you read the experiences of people who were involved in militant struggle that momentarily opened space for liberation—such as the Paris Commune of 1872, the May 1968 uprisings in France, or more recently the George Floyd Uprisings of 2020—there is an out-of-time ecstatic experience of collectivity forged in confronting the state, while also creating the conditions of care that allow for the confrontation to persist. An anarchist understanding of revolution, if we still want to retain that word at all, would be nonlinear. All of these moments are echoes across time—the space of liberation opened time and time again. Similarly, even in our mundane, non-insurrectional lives, we have a scattering of these moments of freedom, of desistance, of refusal, of inattention, and of care that allow anarchism to interject into our now.

Black and Indigenous timelines of resistance also teach us of nonlinear liberation. The linear crush of racial capitalism and state formation that kidnapped Africans and turned them into Black slaves, while displacing and killing Indigenous inhabitants of the stolen lands, met a resistance that often can't be comprehended from a Western understanding of revolution. If the genocide of Indigenous peoples (by states around the world) is an ongoing, multifaceted form of apocalypse, then the asymmetrical warfare that Indigenous people mounted against settlers at every turn would continually carve temporary spaces of liberation and life in the face of the death world that capitalism and the state create. Similarly, Black resistance to chattel slavery wasn't always clear uprising, but other forms of rebellions span coded language, work slowdowns, (sometimes temporary) escapes, reimagined forms of kinship under violent control of social bonds, and marronage, among other ways. I don't hold this history up in order to romanticize the conditions that created the need for finding survival, and beyond that to create and maintain culture under constant siege, but rather to point to the ways that histories of resistance are constantly contemporary—as William C. Anderson shows in *The Nation on No Map*, we need to learn from them and undo the idea that something failed once and for all. Furthermore, the notion of successful revolution may only be apprehended from within a state logic—perhaps then our failures ultimately spell our refusal. Fine-tuning our tactics against state retrenchment, watching the way power imbalances create the splintering that dissolves resistant cultures—this is necessary work. And liberation can't be achieved while the state form continues to exist. But an untimely sense of anarchism can help us draw from reservoirs of insurrectional energy that has created, as the Zapatistas say, a world in which many worlds are possible. In other words, we don't seek to replace a bad world with a good one but to allow for a multifarious way of living for all creatures around the planet.

In their history of southern US rebellion, *Dixie Be Damned*, Saralee Stafford and Neal Shirley propose a discontinuous time of "insurrectionary rupture," building on other anarchist readings of Walter Benjamin's "Theses on the Philosophy of History" and his idea of messianic time. This view of history tries to counter a progressivist or determinist history of revolution, and instead to open, as Stafford and Shirley write, "every moment" to "the potential for the time of this world to end and another to interfere and begin." They connect this to the material experience of participating in moments of insurrection—"refusal, sabotage, or transgression"—where "time stops" and the "social peace" is broken. These interruptions of insurrection testify to the fact that the progressive narrative of history proposed by state and capital is in fact an ongoing war against an actively resistant factor of the world. We receive history on a timeline, but this is a false narrative that can't comprehend the endless forms of life that exceed its capture (or die under its thumb). Thus, for Stafford and Shirley, each moment is not a moment of failure or defeat when the state, through its violent forces, closes down an insurrection, but rather a rift that alters the conditions of reality that unfold afterwards.

Simultaneity: The Intrusion of One World into Another

Anarchism is often dismissed for its inability to last, and yet here it is, popping up at every moment of history under many names, as a countering force to linear time, as a defense against the flattening of narrative, by the texturing of time with multiplicities. As with Anarres, we may think that anarchism's failure would rather be in its lasting— if something was achieved, it would fall back into the same postures of enforcement that new social orders impose. We can instead think of anarchism as a simultaneity, the inability for dreams of freedom to be totally crushed, along with the continual drive for people to alter their social conditions—their relationship with themselves, others, and the world—towards freedom. And this occurs not just in overt moments of struggle but in all the ways that life persists despite attempts to parcel it off into work, family, identity, consumption, and leisure; all of the deadening aspects of administrative life. Anarchist time negates what there is, insofar as it is made to seem inevitable and natural, and opens the ways for the concurrent other ways of being. We are all living anarchist lives in parallel with the official lives we live under the state. We can begin to shift our emphasis, then, on what we consider to be "real" life, so that we can rebuild our relationships and our world.

The novelist Thomas Pynchon has an anarchist character describe this kind of simultaneity as "an anarchist miracle" in *The Crying of Lot 49*: "another world's intrusion into this one." José Arrabal tells the main character, Oedipa Maas: "Most of the time we coexist peacefully, but when we do touch there's cataclysm." This cataclysm is the time of leaderless and spontaneous revolt but also one of effortless collaboration and consensus—the anarchist idea that people tend to organize efficiently without the imposition of order and hierarchy from above. The book goes on to liken this "intrusion of this world into another" to the "kiss of cosmic pool balls," which gives a good sense of the contingency of these moments: a momentary and chance alignment that now produces new paths.

This perspective allows us to counteract a kind of pessimism about the possibility of transformation. There is plenty to be negative about, and the world constantly gets worse and more unlivable. I would go so far as to claim that nihilist views are often necessary to approach the negation of a world order that can knowingly arrange for unlivable life and total environmental destruction. And yet, if we completely ignore the ways that we do survive over and against domination, we fully submit to it (and also lose the energy to rise up in the streets when the moment is right). As I was writing this last line, I saw a car with two bumper stickers: on the left the old revolutionary slogan, "Another World is Possible"; on the right, "Vote like your Rights depended on it." The coexistence of these two slogans in the same place speaks more to me of an intractable pessimism than the thought that nothing can be changed. If your view of the other world is to continually subscribe to the forms of this one—the repeated action of voting to get more abandonment and misery—you should lose hope. Meanwhile, the uprisings that have been cascading across the globe over the last ten years, and even more so in the last few years, should show us that the other life is here now, this is another time, not plotted on a straight line. Following Arrabal's image from *The Crying of Lot 49*, the belief in another possible world is one that constantly exists as interruption; it jumps up into this world of order and violence to resist the onslaught of time.

Reframing the World

Going out in the world with an anarchist perspective means creating or moving every situation towards liberation. We prioritize not just our own self-determination but our mutual need for care and collaboration. Combining what we have patched together from the previous chapters, I want to use this chapter for another perspective shift, towards viewing the world outside the nation state framework so we can map the actual flows of labor, extraction, and destruction that bind most of us together. The major shift we need in our thinking is to let go of the unquestioned goals of humanity and civilization, both of which are invoked in the perpetuation of unsustainable and violent imperial measures. As a culmination, this chapter will put together the anarchist idea of space and time to question the narrative of progress and a human patchwork quilt of competitive nation states with a unified mission of "civilization." The restricted movement of bodies across borders is parodied by the free flow of cash around the world. The ideas of autonomy and mutual aid can help us rethink our places in the world as interlinked groups who can mutually support one another.

Strands in decolonial thinking and the Black radical tradition have made significant moves towards reframing our interrogation of the world by displacing the seemingly neutral terms of humanity and civilization. Anibal Quijano's idea of the "coloniality of power" not only extends the impact of colonialism beyond the concrete practice of colonialism into the very structures of society imposed on Indigenous people and displaced people around the globe through the naturalization of race; in its development by other thinkers, it allows us to see how certain aspects of society—such as gender and humanity itself (see Maria Lugones and Sylvia Wynter)—are naturalized and made to seem eternal. Even down to our bodies, we bear the marks of power, whether we have intimately experienced its violent hand or not. One of the major effects of the expansion of European capitalism across the globe through colonialism and markets has been the standardization of experience, ultimately modeled through consumption and participation in the act of buying. Can we even live our innermost desires as unsullied from those implanted in us by the demand to be woman or man, or to aspire to the aspects of whiteness and beauty and able-bodiedness that vapidly assume the norm through media?

Sylvia Wynter shows that the very concept of Man installed the racialized divisions that exclude sectors of populations from fully attaining the so-called rights that the modern era provided citizens of states with. To put it simply, the whole project of modernity is founded on an anti-Blackness and genocidal colonial project. The spoils of the traffic in bodies and stolen labor fueled the expansion of the capitalist market, underwritten by the strengthening of the violent nation state, then exported around the world in postcolonial movements. Our notion of civic life and politics is fundamentally grounded on a concept of the human, which is not neutral or an abstract idea that just anybody can inhabit, but rather one modeled on racialized and gendered divisions, not to mention class divisions. Man in the abstract is always white man, white cis man, white cisheterosexual able-bodied man. Man is defined through the ability to own property, and property historically has included other people, even if today the law isn't so explicit about it. At the very least, property entails the ability to clear life out of a particular space.

Our whole landscape is premised on these violent exclusions. The history of protest movements has gained minimal concessions and inclusions, but these most often have come in ways of creating further divisions. For example, the Black freedom movement led to the state enabling a Black political class, which helped, on the other side of the actual war the state waged against radical groups, give the sense that Black people in the United States would have representation within the system. William C. Anderson's *The Nation On No Map* describes how the Black freedom movement then itself got universalized as part of the

US narrative, so that the cleaned-up legacy itself ends up belonging to white people to affirm liberal progress narratives and linear time. Of course, this basic sense of identity that the political idea of Man creates, through its racialized and gendered differences, includes the fallacy that sharing a skin color or an assigned gender means sharing interests and needs. This doesn't include distinctions of class, though. A Black political class ends up having more in common with the white ruling class, insofar as they want to maintain their position. They help quell popular unrest through their visibility but can't ultimately change the violent exclusion from within the state structure.

Telling Different Stories

We've entered the discussion around representation in relation to art, figurative representation, and the way that it bleeds into our understanding of bourgeois politics through representative democracy. But our individuality, our identity, is also claimed in this chain of representation—this is seen most clearly with people in marginalized positions. One stands not just as a Black person but a representative of the Black community—and you can say the same thing for queers, women, Latinx, and so on. (For me, this kind of logic was often used in elementary school, where on field trips we were reminded to behave because we represented our school.) As it applies to "minorities," there is pressure to be a model of this identity, otherwise known as "respectability politics." If we act badly or even just air our dirty laundry, it will reflect badly on us—and marginalized groups already have to deal with daily violence doled out by the state, and its condoning of vigilante violence, or even more subtle forms of exclusion. The election of Black representatives, queer/trans representatives, and Indigenous representatives—or intersecting versions of these identities—is intimately tied to the individual's responsibility to represent the community or communities they supposedly belong to (or rather are positioned within by the distribution of power). The top-down focus always erases the networks of care that have made life sustainable in any of these formations, when the few who take the reins of leadership exploit the groups that helped them rise up.

We might extend this representative quality to the mission of humanity and civilization, in light of how Wynter discusses this era where our species dominates the planet. We are representative of humanity, who have God-given dominion over the earth. But in the same way that rights discourse has historically deflated rebellion against racism, homophobia, misogyny, and other forms of oppression, the invocation of humanity to protect so-called human rights in the ongoing and continuous record of genocidal state actions proves to be largely useless. We talk about humanity as a sort of goal or aim, the arc of progress, the Enlightenment and escape from dark ages: violence and brutality is in the past, and our future is peace, technology, and coexistence. And yet, this narrative conveniently smooths over the fact that the brutality of the past is ongoing, and the past contains many pockets of more equitable, peaceful, just ways of living than racial capitalism and competing nation states. And still the narrative prioritizes competition, selfishness, and personal gain, all at the expense of cooperation and help.

The progress myth of humanity and civilization is an ongoing process of domestication, bringing us and the world under control. It is a universal and totalizing project that intends to dominate all corners of the earth. However, the aim for totalization will always leave gaps. The problem then is to find the escape routes, not necessarily in the old 1960s mode of "dropping out," but perhaps merely in the parts of life that are ungoverned and ungovernable. The anarchist perspective here is important as a countermeasure to the universalizing invocations of humanity as a supposed ethics, an invocation for a certain decorum of behavior. Anarchism would be a non-universalizing ethics, one that promotes liberation, self-determination, care, multiple ways of living simultaneously, no correct method, harm reduction, letting go, the end.

But how do we divest ourselves of the horrible weight of humanity and civilization? Social contract theory—whether the seemingly benign Rousseau version of trading one freedom for another or the darker Hobbes version of consenting to be governed in order to receive protection from brutality—imagines an outside, a place ostensibly of possible escape. They posit "natural" life outside of society, outside civilization, outside the state, and create a narrative of our submission to a form of control, ostensibly out of a (collective?) self-interest. And yet the actual function of state society is to close down and whittle away any image or possibility of outside, to remove us from the things that make life possible, so we can focus on the things that make profits. The coexisting stateless societies are painted as relics of an immemorial past at best, or tainted with the brush of depravity and want for not measuring up to the modern technological comforts that the state-sponsored nuclear family/wage-earning relationships foster. One of the major ways this happens is through the naturalization or normalization of the conditions inside society—with the effect that outside and inside are no longer distinguishable. In other words, human nature is unchangeable, as natural as the world, and only gets modified and maximized through increasing levels of organization—or rather hierarchical power structures. Another way that people are kept enclosed in society is to perpetuate the notion that whatever the outside might offer, it is not worth giving up what you have inside. I think of this as the "will we have Netflix after the revolution/apocalypse?" conundrum, where the thought of losing a minor luxury that helps maintain our current complacency keeps us from imagining a vastly better world outside of the state and market.

Naturalization and myths of progress are modes of capitalist and statist ideology. However, anarchism isn't a counter-ideology that would replace this mode of totalization with another. Anarchism doesn't want a total system. Instead it's a flexible way of thinking that tries to navigate from one impossibility to another through an amalgamation of aims of letting be, increasing freedom, and strengthening actual bonds through care. Anarchism is a practice, we do it everyday.

Leap into the Unknown

So the answer to the question "how will it work?" is that it won't. Not at first, not always. And it won't be work in the sense we understand it. We will always risk failure, something every militant is familiar with.

But we can think of failure in the queer mode, as Jack Halberstam has framed it, as an opting out of capitalist narratives of success that normalize particular ways of life. The refrain of this book is to break up the things that don't work so you can envision other possible ways. It's a process of experimentation. This book proposes another notion of time where every moment doesn't have to be maximized into forever. Think about this as a contradiction of Kantian ethics, which says that every action I take must be thought of as a possible rule for everyone's behavior. Instead, an anarchist ethics takes every action in itself, faces the consequences, and admits the possibility of error. The Kantian ethics is violent. The anarchist ethics doesn't preclude violence but allows space to confront it through repair and care.

The other refrain of this book is an invitation to shift perspective, thus allowing a reimagining of the landscape we inhabit outside of its ordered layout. Though there is a certain seduction in how conspiracy theories try to unmask the real world through manipulative lies, such as the way the alt right seized on the metaphor of pills from the *Matrix*, this metaphor is a simplification. Even a film such as *They Live*—where the protagonist finds a pair of glasses that allow him to see the subliminal messages that control behavior through state and media in an apocalyptic USA—oversimplifies the process I am suggesting here, which is more like a kaleidoscope shift than a full-on replacement of one world with another. The *Matrix* allegory can be traced back to anarchist aligned theorization, from Jean Baudrillard's simulacrum to Guy Debord's society of the spectacle, which theorize that the current stage of capitalism replaces society with an image of itself: a highly mediated form of engagement that removes people from their environment and social bonds with others. Even a liberal political thinker, Hannah Arendt, theorized this as "image making," in response to the US government and media representation of the war in Vietnam. In her work, this total replacement of facts with an image of the world is a development of totalitarianism or fascism, which will be unrecognizable from earlier iterations. We are living now in an even more developed version of this world—Netflix again is a good example, especially in pandemic/lockdown life for those of us living in a postindustrial state with an internet connection. You can replace your interaction with the world with narratives of it. Your consumption of media even seems to allow you to express your political convictions. And we can find revisionist histories of the world where social problems are neutralized or easily survivable (this is Frederic Jameson's version of utopia in mass media, where the narrative solves a social problem, ultimately alleviating the viewer from any responsibility of action).

The anarchist kaleidoscope shift doesn't uncover a secret truth like a conspiracy theory. The thing you learn when you start to analyze the world from a critical anarchist perspective is how blatant and explicit these modes of manipulation and oppression are. There is no secret, and it's not a conspiracy: it's the way this world functions. But the conspiracy mindset does point symptomatically to the fact that many people feel that the world is totally wrong; that our lives are lived in a way that doesn't actually make sense and serves almost no one. The kaleidoscope shift then lets us look at our own lives and our own desires. It permits us to live our desires outside the confines that have predetermined pathways of inclusion and exclusion, both of which are forms of violence. And it permits us to leave when we are done.

The Rhythm of Revolutionary Time

This book was completed in 2022, a vantage point from which the Covid-19 pandemic appears to have fundamentally altered our experience of time. Lockdown time. Work from home, no childcare time. Timelines of knowledge, misinformation, discovery, waiting for a vaccine, counting deaths. And all the while, essential work time for many—continued service at risk of life. Finally, return to normal time, forget it, it's over—a version of Trump's nostalgic fallacy, "Make America Great Again"—in the end, it's all contradictory time, trying to hold two opposing things in the mind at once. Return to what? I had hoped the contradiction of being forced to pay bills while not being able to work would make people refuse. Pandemic time is a loss of time, and in the end it led to uprising time, a bubbling over.

The potential for revolutionary perspective came in waves, as it always does. Our waves must meet the boom and bust of capitalist crisis, which is either temporarily staved off or hastened by internal and external factors. The sense of timelessness, or the linear march of progression, distracts us from the fact that we are always relatively unstable. It's like an abusive relationship, in which the desperate need to get your footing, catch your breath, overwhelms your ability to escape the patterns of abuse. Thus, we are built up, kept hopeful, and then slammed down and destroyed periodically. For those of us who entered adulthood during the time of the 2008 market crash, for those of us who were facing the bribe of the bourgeois lifestyle of career, family, accumulation of wealth, retirement—we have the concrete example of those illusions being swept out of reach. And thus, we have also had the experience of innovating new methods of survival in the managed chaos of state and market, which rules our lives according to their own 24/7 timeline. However, to manage our own survival often means endless work, being constantly available, a dwindling away of rest, of recuperation, and a serious decline of health.

At this point, the fact of massive abandonment by the state—and the job market—for most across the capitalist core is so glaring that we should see that the crumbling of institutions is inevitable. Pair this with the upsurge of environmental catastrophe, which is getting worse every year but also coming in waves and unevenly spread around the world, and we can only acclimatize ourselves to the dissolution of the institutions that have posed as lasting, like the state and economy. Politicians and corporations continually propose market solutions to the problems, but those have also proven not to work, only hastening the collapse that will leave us in an unrecognizable situation, be it one of increased terror and abandonment or, as we rather hope, a situation of unprecedented care and freedom. The time that this crumbling creates, in the retreat of social services by the state, is the increased securitized services resulting in a massive boom in prison populations: people doing time, a slow death.

On the one hand, anarchists want to hasten a certain end: the end of rule and domination. The end always seems to entail destruction and violence of different kinds. And many anarchists would acknowledge that there will be no change of order without violent confrontation. The state may abandon us to waste away, but they won't abandon their stranglehold on power, the ability to put people to death, or mete out bare survival for many. As Frantz Fanon insisted, the program of decolonization means "total disorder."

But as the development of capitalism and the rise of nation states has been an uneven process that is still unfinished, we can no longer hope for the punctual revolution. Instead, we can only anticipate a conflict on many fronts and many timelines at once: discontinuous, disappointing, and hopeful; not additive but fractal or exponential. So on the other hand, while we want to hasten the end—and know when to end things—we also have to maintain an experimental approach to keep trying, even in the face of failure (the failure that is caused by the co-optation of the state, the loss of funds, the burnout of participants, the messiness of relationships), and then learn from the kinds of failure that harm our chances to continue to care for ourselves, to survive into the unknown future.

After reading this, whether or not you feel drawn to using the term anarchism, my hope is that you will be inspired to experiment and improvise with these practices to see how you can infuse your daily life with a feeling of liberation, and from there to form new entanglements with others and the world.

FAQs

Will the revolution ever come? Aren't we always losing?

With the ever more apparent destruction of the planet, the rise of worldwide fascism, and increasing precarity for most of us, it's hard not to lose hope and see throughout the last 500 years of history a general trend towards human destruction. I would argue that even the desire for revolution as a punctual event that topples the social order in one go is a genocidal urge that necessarily includes mass death. Perhaps looking at history from a distance, it seems like the people are always losing out to power—but this grand view misses all the moments of resistance, insurrection, and self-defense, not to mention the ways that people have improvised and maintained lives of joy in the midst of terror. Another side to anarchism—beyond bringing about situations of confrontation with power through direct action—is enacting the social relations of mutuality and care that will form a liberated world. We can do that now in all of our interactions, from this moment till after the revolution!

Does what I do matter?

Our little actions do matter! Capitalism needs workers, the state needs citizens who comply. Our individual and collective refusal to enact the behaviors and modes of life demanded of us to fit their mold are so many cracks in their system that aims at totality. We can't wait for a top-down approach to changing the world; that idea relies on state logics of a central hierarchy that makes decisions. We change the world here and now in every moment, and our actions form the better world we want. Prioritize care over work, joy over duty, excess over dwindling returns. Take your energy out of making their world and make your own! Anarchism lies in all the minute refusals, the concrete acts we do to prioritize living over survival.

Coda: No Place, or Living in a World Without a State

An early scene in Le Guin's *The Dispossessed* shows Shevek, the anarchist physicist and interplanetary traveler, as an infant pushing another child out of his sunny spot on the floor of the nursery. Shevek is literally fighting for his "place in the sun," the phrase that accompanied Germany's aggressive colonial politics at the end of the nineteenth century. What Le Guin does so perfectly in this scene is to address head on the myth of nasty and competitive human nature and its tension with the process of socialization and the scene of care. The adult minding the children in the nursery scolds Shevek but she also picks him up and holds him. When Shevek says, "mine sun," she explains that no one owns it, that it is there to share. His aggression, a blind response to sharing space unthinkingly, is met with a reinforcement of commonality.

When Georges Bataille aims to displace the capitalist fallacy of scarcity and the exchange-based market economy, he uses the sun's unceasing outpouring of energy and light as the metaphor for his general economy, which runs on unproductive expenditure and unnecessary wastes of energy. The sun shines on (until it doesn't) with generosity. Though the surface of the world limits the space available for using this energy, there is still plenty of sun to go around, for Shevek and his playmate and for all of us. At least for now.

Enclosures exist to reinforce that limited sense of space, a scarcity that makes us worry about resources, survival, and even the possibility of love. Even in a common room, you start to feel that you have your spot, your favorite seat. But this is where utopian thinking—utopia in its root sense—comes in handy. No place. When I want to reinforce my sense of possibility (of resistance) in this world—a possibility that usually has to be thought of in terms of escape—the thought of no place as our place takes me there. It's not nowhere or nonexistent. Neither is it Nowheresville, a reference to the domination of a centralized society, where the hierarchy of city over country or the colonial framework of metropole and periphery holds sway. That is the kind of prejudice that can turn no place into a wasteland.

Oscar Wilde wrote that "a map of the world that does not include utopia is not worth glancing at." The idea of mapping gets at the overwhelming feeling of confinement that can shut down utopian thinking (or wishing, or working, or planning). If the world has been mapped, then perhaps there is no escape. When mapping fueled colonial projects, the romantic notion that veiled the exercise in domination was an encounter with the unknown. At the other end of geographical imperialism, in today's surveillance state and in the wake of the totalitarian dream of everyone in their place, we have a sense of inevitability that we carry around with us. We may feel, if not that the world has already been entirely plotted out (which means all the places are already owned), then at least that our place within the world has been pinpointed, our thoughts censored, our resistance contained.

The structure of this stage of capitalism extends the imperial mapping project from the surface of the world to all the structures, beings, feelings, and ideas that roam around on it. It tells us the future is written, resistance is futile. Cities are built so that the world feels small. Not like a "small town," where everyone knows each other: in cities, we are unknown individuals, but there is no other world. When the city does try to replicate the "small town" feeling, it does so in a highly commodified form geared towards tourism. The remapping of the big city as the small town tourist paradise occurs under the guise of security, policing populations and ensuring the eternal separation of the people who live there and the people who visit.

Simply leaving the city, wandering in the woods, one can easily combat this feeling. That may sound romantic in itself, but there the towering trees, the noisy silence—crisp leaves crunching, hushed cascades pouring down, buzzing insects invisibly whirring—remind you that the world is actually enormous. Just like the sun, there is plenty to go around, enough to provide the means of living. Your body strikes a balance in scale. A world without a nation is a world that is not made "to the measure of man," the old narcissistic, patriarchal dream of philosophers and poets. A world without states is a world that holds humans and all other beings on its surface to share in the plenty that it can provide. This feeling can happen even in the urban environment, no matter how much it is structured to isolate us and break possibilities of solidarity. (Of course, those forces work with another kind of vehemence in rural settings too.)

I want to rewrite anarchism into the here and now as marking these spaces that are no place: not mapped, located, cornered, or ordered. Even our bodies are marked with internal surveillance. But we always know moments of freedom, the sense that no one is watching. A post-state world translates those internal freedoms into physical space, where we live uncontained. Every place is no place, even wherever it is you call home. We don't feel crowded when we realize the sun pours incessantly and we won't get pushed aside.

In *Times Square Red, Times Square Blue*, Delany imagines a version of this within the late-capitalist state, spaces that counter the ongoing class struggle. They are public spaces where people of different classes make contact. His main example is the porn theater in Times Square from the 1960s to the 1990s, where people of various backgrounds could meet for consensual sex acts and maybe conversation. However, Delany reminds us that such spaces are always under threat by the structure of class warfare and must be perennially reopened. Part of this fight, he writes, happens in language and how we talk about things.

One of the most powerful tools of shutting down open space—to populate no place and enclose the commons—happens through the cynical claim that "this is the way things are." It also works to say: this is just where we are, we can't help it. But we can prefigure our liberation in the powerful moments of freedom that constantly occur—when fragile yet totalizing ideology loosens its grasp on our bodies and minds. The feeling lets us know that the other world is already here and the sun is shining on everyone equally. We are there when we know we have what we need, that most of what we have we don't really want; we are there when we feel the world expand its surface and we are overshadowed by a tree trunk, or fall asleep in the breezy shade of a rocky cliff, when you sit on a porch in a town or a city and you know that you aren't actually there, at the intersection of such and such streets, but on the edge of a series of infinite interlocking circles.

On the one hand, I am arguing that utopia is here and now, because it is no place, and therefore can't be gridded onto a propertarian view of the world. If we gather those liberating moments of nowhere, we have enough ground to stand on to realize a world without a nation, a world built on care where we can hear one another at last. But this also seems like it requires some kind of accumulation of moments, which fits within the oppressive paradigm of capitalism. Therefore, on the other hand, what these fleeting moments of freedom show us is that a world without a nation, a world where everyone is free, is not static. It needs to be renewed again and again by telling alternative histories.

It is clear that to believe that everything is mapped and owned and located is also to allow there to be vast empty spaces that are unaccounted for, like the tortured child in the basement in Le Guin's *Omelas*, whose horrific condition allows for the blissful denial of the community. Living in a state, we avoid responsibility by assuming that someone else will take care of us. This creates a twisted sense of freedom: that what we really want is to be let off the hook from caring. But, in reality, freedom means care; it means recognizing the power of the moments of absence from the world regime that we may experience daily, and working from there to face our conflicts together.

Without a state, we will have nothing to contradict our experience of no place, as these moments continuously happen, by forcing us to attest to a world where nothing changes, everyone has their place, and it could never be any other way. Still, when we achieve the stateless society, we will not suddenly be let off the hook. We will still be here, nowhere, and we will be here with each other, with all of our needs and desires. In a stateless society, space is made for no place. We each already live there, alone and together, certain of the incredible vastness of the world, which promises its plenty and our ultimate freedom, and amid the close quarters of sharing sunshine, whose excess gives us a model for living together in a world without borders. There the play of light and shadow is not threatening; they do not match up with good and evil, but instead both enable us to be beyond.

Further Reading

What follows is an incomplete list of suggested texts for further reading. I selected some texts that influenced my writing here, though this is by no means exhaustive. Any contribution I make is indebted to the work of these authors and many more unnamed here (though some mentioned through the text).

Black Feminism

The Combahee River Collective statement is one of the most important political documents ever written, providing a Black feminist theory of coalitional politics that should inspire contemporary anarchists.

bell hooks argues for "theory as liberatory practice" in *Teaching to Transgress: Education as the Practice of Freedom.* She cautions that theory can be used for good or ill, and so a liberatory commitment means priming theory for the ends you envision. All of bell hooks's work is important further reading!

Audre Lorde, the Black lesbian feminist warrior poet, is essential reading. You can start with *Sister Outsider,* a collection of her most famous essays and speeches.

Saidiya Hartman's *Wayward Lives, Beautiful Experiments: Intimate Histories of Riotous Black Girls, Troublesome Women, and Queer Radicals* is a masterpiece and a huge influence on my thinking of discovering everyday anarchism outside of the structures of European political thinking. Hartman's other work is also incredibly important for thinking about the legacies of slavery and colonialism.

Indigenous/Decolonial Texts

Frantz Fanon's *Black Skin, White Masks* and *The Wretched of the Earth* are essential reading for understanding the processes of colonization and the project of decolonization.

Gord Hill's *500 Years of Indigenous Resistance* retells the history of European colonization of the Americas from the point of view of Indigenous armed struggle against the invaders.

Two important essays co-authored by Eve Tuck help define decolonization and Indigenous feminism by looking at the structure of settler colonialism (rather than thinking of colonization as a past event): "Decolonizing Feminism: Challenging Connections between Settler Colonialism and Heteropatriarchy" (2013) by Maile Arvin, Eve Tuck, and Angie Morrill and "Decolonization Is Not a Metaphor" (2012) by Eve Tuck and K. Wayne Yang.

Mississauga Nishnaabeg writer Leanne Betasamosake Simpson's *As We Have Always Done: Indigenous Freedom through Radical Resistance* is very influential for my thinking of practical anarchism, as she frames a project not of revolution but resurgence of the lifeways that settler colonialism has tried to erase through war, genocide, and the production of knowledge.

Anarchism

Russell "Maroon" Shoatz, a member of the Black Liberation Army, was imprisoned from 1972 until his death in December 2021. His writing collected in *Maroon the Implacable* details the historical resistance of enslaved Black people and Africans, specifically in maroon societies, which organized life outside of the dominant system while also raiding and liberating people on the inside.

Saralee Stafford and Neal Shirley's *Dixie Be Damned: 300 Years of Insurrection in the American South* details a history of resistance in the South from an anarchist perspective, telling counterhistories to dominant narratives.

Zoé Samudzi and William C. Anderson's *As Black as Resistance* as well as Anderson's recent *The Nation on No Map* provide essential contemporary insight into Black anarchism.

Lorenzo Kom'Boa Ervin's classic text, *Anarchism and the Black Revolution*, is an important development of Black anarchism out of the Black liberation movement of the mid-twentieth century.

Colin Ward's *Anarchy in Action*, first published in 1973, still retains its accessible overview of anarchistic modes of living and organizing the world. Ward uses overlooked and local examples of self-management and community organization to disprove the old tale that authority is necessary to get things done.

Peter Gelderloos has written two important books that offer important introductions to anarchism: *Anarchy Works* and *Worshipping Power*. Both books detail ways of life outside of state society, along with how different people have resisted the violent imposition of state structures on their lifeways and access to resources.

Cindy Milstein's *Anarchism and Its Aspirations* twins history with theory to argue that anarchism is in fact a crucial intervention in freedom movements for our current time. Milstein's more recent books are also helpful practical anarchist texts: *Rebellious Mourning* and *Nothing So Whole as a Broken Heart* collect essays on mourning, collective ritual through Jewish anarchism, and the centering of care as a necessary aspect of our movement.

carla bergman and Nick Montgomery's *Joyful Militancy* counters rigid thinking in radical circles, avoiding nihilistic or macho adherence to a singular view of struggle, and imbuing militancy with a sense of joy—not frivolous happiness, but the collective work of care and world-building that enables any kind of large-scale resistance.

All of David Graeber's work provides accessible anarchist entry points. My favorite, *Fragments of an Anarchist Anthropology*, builds from histories of counterpower in colonized societies, where people lived outside the state while not actively confronting it, discusses the different economic ideas based on the gift, and develops a theory of revolution outside the punctual event of superb violence.

Eli Meyerhoff's *Beyond Education: Radical Studying for Another World* provides an anarchist take on the education system and schooling through historical examples of schools breaking liberatory movements as well as alternative studying practices in and outside of institutions.

Vicky Osterweil's *In Defense of Looting: A Riotous History of Uncivil Action* reframes people's resistance, with most focus on Black uprisings in the USA, through the radical act of looting, as an important anti-capitalist, anti-racist, liberatory practice.

Abolition/Transformative Justice

adrienne maree brown's work on "emergent strategy," developed in her book of the same name and the following collection, *Pleasure Activism*, along with subsequent installments on community accountability. brown writes from within the Black feminist tradition of prison abolition and transformative justice, and is one of the more prominent voices in the current practice of rethinking accountability to ourselves and our loved ones, alongside other networks of care that relate to birthing, illness, and death.

Mariame Kaba is a long-term prison abolitionist and community accountability facilitator who analyzes the failure of state institutions to reduce harm, particularly for Black people, and provides roadmaps and workbooks enabling communities to work together to resolve conflict and respond to harm. She has created guidebooks to implement transformative methods of conflict resolution, as well as collected essays on the complimentary work of abolition and transformation. See Mariame Kaba, *We Do This 'Til We Free Us: Abolitionist Organizing and Transforming Justice*, and Mariame Kaba and Shira Hassan, *Fumbling towards Repair: A Workbook for Community Accountability Facilitators*.

In *Care Work: Dreaming Disability Justice*, Leah Lakshmi Piepzna-Samarasinha writes from a disabled perspective about the forms of innovative care that people excluded from access to the "normal" world necessarily create.

Dean Spade and Tourmaline made a series of videos for the Barnard Center for Research on Women that provides an extremely helpful introduction to prison abolition and transformative justice: "No One Is Disposable: Everyday Practices of Prison Abolition" (https://bcrw.barnard.edu/videos/reina-gossett-dean-spade-no-one-is-disposable-online-discussion/).

Other Feminist Texts

Silvia Federici's manifesto, *Wages against Housework*, greatly inspired my thinking here. Her book, *Caliban and the Witch: Women, the Body and Primitive Accumulation*, tells the story of the violent imposition of capitalism through the gendered division of labor.

Donna Haraway's "Cyborg Manifesto" was an influential feminist intervention into ideas of technology, nature, and liberation that still has lessons for us today.

Sophie Lewis is a contemporary thinker of feminism and family abolition. Her book *Full Surrogacy Now! Feminism against the Family* builds on Haraway and Federici in innovative ways.

Valerie Solanas's *SCUM Manifesto*, while outrageous, envisions an anarchist utopia without the problem of men. It is one of my favorite texts.

Queer Texts

Guy Hocquenghem's writings are hugely important for anti-capitalist theories of gay liberation.

Monique Wittig's writing articulates a gender abolitionism through lesbian feminism.

Larry Mitchell's *The Faggots and Their Friends between Revolutions* is a classic queer mythology of revolution from the gay liberation period.

All of the queer nihilist work by *baedan* provides important critiques of gendered civilization and theories of insurrectionary anarchism.

Cathy Cohen's "Punks, Bulldaggers, and Welfare Queens" is an important intervention into the pitfalls of queer identity politics without an understanding of building solidarity.

Science Fiction

Two anarchist science fiction novels, originally published in the 1970s, are still very helpful exercises in thinking through the benefits and problems of organizing society along anarchist lines: Ursula K. Le Guin's *The Dispossessed*, and Marge Piercy's *Woman on the Edge of Time*.

The speculative work of Samuel Delany and Octavia Butler, while not necessarily envisioning anarchist worlds, provides complex narratives of power, desire, and difference that can help us think about the world-building we want to do here and now.

There is a growing library of radical speculative/science fiction—especially work by Black/Indigenous/queer/trans writers. I like Rivers Solomon, Margaret Killjoy, adrienne maree brown, Adi Callai, and Alan Lea. Go find it!

Acknowledgments

To Kerry, who taught me the anarchism of loving (and) parenting and who helped me really see life can be any way you want. You have believed in me in so many of the things I have undertaken; I am here because of you. You may not realize, but your critical vision continually helps me rethink my views about the world. Your art and the poetry of your words have opened my eyes to new interactions of shape, beauty, and life. To Bella, who also has taught me anarchism in everyday interactions. Knowing you has forced me to check my own authoritarian impulses. You truly bring me joy in my life. I am inspired by your wildness, your creativity, your snuggles, and your puns!

Bursts O' Goodness was an early reader of my proposal and my draft, not to mention he has helped me work out ideas in discussion and action for the last number of years, a true friend and comrade. E Ornelas was also an early reader of the manuscript with a helpful critical eye that helped me finetune my ideas. I have been in conversation and collaboration with E and Kai Rajala over the last few years, trying to rethink anarchism and its relationship to utopia. I am thankful to have two comrades in thought like E and Kai. Zakir Paul has been a longtime confidant and dear friend; I am ever grateful that you have stuck out this infinite conversation with me. Eli Meyerhoff read my chapter on education and with detailed notes helped me strengthen my thinking there. I have learned so much collaborating with Eli and the other people working on Abolitionist University Studies. Raechel Anne Jolie gave a careful read of the initial manuscript with many helpful notes, plus more feedback along the way—but moreover, has been an essential interlocuter on many of the ideas I have presented here. Thank you for being willing to hold the complexities in conversation with me, that's so rare! My friend and collaborator Amar has a flexible way of thinking of anarchism and queerness and everything, I am always learning from our conversations. Working with MB on projects is always my favorite, we work well together. Brian D. first asked me to write the chapter on art that I reworked for the book. He has also taught me so much through conversation and talks. I was first inspired by him in my ideas of dissolution. I collaborated with Margaret Killjoy on community workshops envisioning better worlds, which really helped me consider practical details in a new way. She has also often visited my classes to be another voice for anarchy with my science fiction students. I originally conceived the coda in response to a call for writing that Margaret and Strangers in a Tangled Wilderness put out. Jamie Theophilos has collaborated with me on workshops, lectures, and punk music. We are in an ongoing conversation about how accountability might ever work, and why punk is the way it is. We'll figure it out, I'm sure. Grier Low is my favorite gay book nerd, who always has amazing recommendations that open my brain back up. Melissa González has used her access to resources to support me with work in my most difficult moments, she is a role model for radical study in the university. I've been lucky to collaborate with glo merriweather, Ash Williams, and Jamie Marsicano on multiple occasions. They are all amazing teachers, who show up for the real moments too. Firestorm Books in Asheville grounded me in flight and the current and former members of the collective have given me space to share ideas and create community. Thank you also to all the people I have organized with, processed conflict with, dreamt of life with. I also have to thank my students, who read along with me and try to understand the world, share their perspectives, and look for ways to fight back. My sister, my mother, my father, my grandmother, have all given me support and space in all my difficulties over all the years.

Ken Barlow at Pluto Press was looking for a book like this, and I felt like I could offer a good take on anarchism as a daily practice. I am grateful that Ken saw something in my proposal, and I was lucky to have his editorial eye on the drafts as they developed into this book. Thank you for believing in the project, here it is!

Thanks to our Patreon subscribers:

Andrew Perry
Ciaran Kane

Who have shown generosity and
comradeship in support of our publishing.

Check out the other perks you get by subscribing
to our Patreon – visit patreon.com/plutopress.

Subscriptions start from £3 a month.

The Pluto Press Newsletter

Hello friend of Pluto!

Want to stay on top of the best radical books
we publish?

Then sign up to be the first to hear about our
new books, as well as special events,
podcasts and videos.

You'll also get 50% off your first order with us
when you sign up.

Come and join us!

Go to bit.ly/PlutoNewsletter